Skypilot

Memoirs from Take-off to Landing

PETER GRAHAM

Pentland Books
Edinburgh – Cambridge – Durham – USA

First published in 2001 by
Pentland Books
1 Hutton Close
South Church
Bishop Auckland
Durham

sales@pentlandpress.co.uk
manuscripts@pentlandpress.co.uk
www.pentlandpress.co.uk

ISBN 1-85821-909-4

Typeset in AdobeGaramond 11 on 13 by
Carnegie Publishing
Carnegie House
Chatsworth Road
Lancaster

www.carnegiepub.co.uk
www.wooof.net

Printed and bound by
Antony Rowe Ltd
Chippenham

INTRODUCTION

The title Skypilot is chosen because that was what in the RAF we called our chaplain or, for that matter, any other minister of religion.

When I was thirteen I decided I wanted to be a Spitfire pilot. I reached this objective when I was twenty. Until I was twenty-six I used to swear black and blue that under no circumstances would I ever be a 'bloody parson'. But by the time I was thirty I'd become what I swore I'd never be – a skypilot.

My wartime experience was often exciting, sometimes painful, occasionally terrifying. It was all compressed into four years. I have been fortunate enough to have had not altogether dissimilar experiences in the rest of my life but with a great deal of joy as well.

I make no claim to historical accuracy in these memoirs. I tell my tale as best as I can remember it with the help of a few friends and relations. As I look back from old age this is how I see it. I trust I will be forgiven by those I refer to if I've written anything they find disagreeable or untrue.

Just after the end of the war in Europe I returned to England believing that all my fellow pilots of 41 Squadron had been killed except those who had been prisoners of war like me. I was enormously relieved to discover this was quite untrue. They were a wonderful lot and it's great to know that most of them are still going strong.

CHAPTER I

In spite of all efforts to recapture the experience, I've no idea what my birth was like. It happened in Oxford on 11 April 1923. Judging by remarks made from time to time by my mother, all the births of her six children were very distressing. She loved her children wonderfully but made no bones about the difficulty she had bringing us into the world.

At that time my father was Dean of Oriel College, where he had been as an undergraduate. In spite of his slight stature he had rowed for his college and even at one time been in the university trial eight. He never showed the least disappointment that none of his sons became oarsmen, though the youngest did go to Oriel. My mother was a graduate of Lady Margaret Hall, where she had been captain of boats. This distinction meant that she could take out a college boat whenever she liked for the rest of her life. Her preference was for punting; as a result of which we all eventually learned that art.

It may well be that it was something to do with this parentage that the whole family had a love of water. Since throughout our childhood we lived almost as far as possible from the sea that meant we were absorbed in our local river and in small streams. These we used to dam so that various minor canals and streams could be built with working waterwheels made of sticks and string. This occupation came to be called 'watergoes'. Whenever we indulged in it we used to come home covered in mud but very happy; nor were we ever reprimanded by our parents for this.

When I was three and had a one-year-old sister, Mary, as well as my older brother, John, we moved to Boyton in Wiltshire where my father was the incumbent of three small parishes. Boyton Rectory where we lived was a splendid house with extensive garden and a paddock beyond. There were steep banks round the lawn and it was possible to roll down them and get thoroughly giddy in the process. We burned logs on the hearth in our drawing room and I remember my surprise when reading a Beatrix Potter book to discover that this sort of fire was unusual. That was in the 1920s. Now of course a log fire is enjoyed by far more people.

At Christmas time we had a magnificent tree bedecked with real candles, which were lit at least once on Christmas Day. The rectory had electricity for lighting but not for anything else. The power came from a petrol engine in the scullery and it enthralled me chiefly because its exhaust pipe chugged out noxious fumes into the passage leading to our backyard.

We had a pure white and very gentle bull terrier. I used to ride on his back from time to time.

My mother also taught us the elements of astronomy, getting us to study the stars at night and giving us a fair understanding of the Solar System. This she accomplished by planting a football outside our front door, saying 'That's the Sun. Now we'll go for a walk and I'll show you where the planets fit in.' So, armed with an orange to represent Jupiter, several marbles of various sizes, silver balls and hundreds and thousands from the kitchen, we went out planting these 'planets' around the countryside at what I suppose were roughly the appropriate distances from each other and from the Sun.

My first experience of motherly care that I did not think of as perfectly loving happened when I had a nasty fall when running down a steepish hill in the road just by the rectory. Screaming at the top of my voice, I arrived in our garden to be met by mother, who took a quick look at the gash in my knee and bade me wait while she fetched the fitting remedy. Very soon she was back with a bottle of iodine which she splashed liberally on my knee. I guess my screams then were even louder than before and I no longer believed mother was always going to be good to me.

When I had just turned six my father was made Vicar of Cuddesdon and Principal of the famous theological college there. While our parents were settling in with the two youngest children, Mary and Stephen, who was still a small baby, John and I spent a few days with our maternal grandparents in their lovely house, Beechwood, in Iffley on the edge of Oxford. A day or two later we were put on the bus for Cuddesdon. There was no one on board but the driver and ourselves and we much enjoyed the journey, tearing up and down the bus and occasionally admiring the scenery with which we were to become so familiar since Cuddesdon was to be our home for the next fifteen years. It was a very attractive village with a marvellous Norman church.

Here we lived in some style, though I suppose it was less grand than that of some of our predecessors. I deduce this from the fact that one of the first things my parents organised was the turning of three maids' bedrooms into one large room to be our nursery. That left us with just one bedroom for our two living-in servants, cook and house-parlour maid. For most of our time there we had a nanny who was a local young woman coming in each day and staying until we were in bed. We had a fulltime gardener and sometimes a boy to assist him. On top of all these now and again we'd have a governess. One such was Aza Obolensky, who had two claims to fame for us: first, she was a Russian princess, second, she had a brother who was a most distinguished wing three-quarter for Oxford University Rugby Club. My biggest spectator thrill ever was seeing him run the whole length of the field to score a try against Cambridge.

At Cuddesdon religion became very important. My parents saw to it that Sunday was both a day for worship and also the happiest day of the week. We had a strict regime over sweets, being allowed just one a day after lunch. On Fridays and other Fast days of the Church no sweets were allowed, whereas on Sundays and Saints' days the ration was doubled. On Sundays in college term time we were also allowed to come down in dressing gowns after our nightly bath and join in the 'Bright Hour'. This ran from 8.30 to 9.30 p.m. and was devoted chiefly to songs sung by students of the College. These tended to be amusing pieces but all sorts of music were put on and occasionally someone would just tell a funny story.

My parents were in church every day of the week and on Sundays my mother would be at an 8 a.m. Communion and back again for Matins and Eucharist at 11, finishing the worship round with 6.30 Evensong. When we were very small mother would skip Matins and take us in to the service just in time for the Sung Eucharist. That was the only service we were allowed to go to. As we got older we would plead to be allowed to come with her to Evensong. I'm sure I was often bored by parts of all this but it felt grown-up to be doing what the adults did.

On top of this church-going we had family prayers every weekday after breakfast. This was compulsory for the whole household. Papa would expound some passage of scripture and lead us in set prayers. All this seemed perfectly natural and the same routine was followed when we stayed at Beechwood; only there we didn't have a chapel but prayed in the dining room, the worship being led with great dignity by Granhardy.

Soon after our arrival at Cuddesdon I had my first mystical experience. I was standing on the terrace on the south side of the vicarage with a lawn in front of me and shrubberies ahead and on both sides. It was a lovely summer's day and as I looked up at the fleecy white clouds sailing overhead there was a dramatic change in my perception. This is hard to put into words but I've often tried to describe it. The best I can do is to say that it was as if the scene before me had changed from black and white to glorious Technicolor. At the same time I felt suddenly warmer; it was the kind of warmth I associate with being firmly but gently hugged by someone much loved. I saw no face; I heard no voice but felt absolutely certain that I was loved and accepted by whatever was meant by 'God'.

CHAPTER II

The vicarage had eight bedrooms, my father's dressing room, two bathrooms, five reception rooms and the well-known green baize door dividing the family's part of the house from the servants' quarters. Beyond this door were two steps down and then on the left the pantry, the back stairs and the boot room plus WC, while on the right were the boiler room, the kitchen, the storeroom, the larder and the scullery.

The garden was in three parts. In front of the house there was the tennis lawn and also a circular area of rough grass dominated by a great beech tree in the middle. There was a flower border round the edge of this area and in it were two buddleia bushes which used to attract swarms of butterflies in the season. During college term time we were not allowed in this part of the garden except between lunch and tea. This was to ensure that our childish shouts would not disturb the students who would be working in the college on the far side of this front garden

Here we played tennis and cricket. For much of the time John and I would be the cricketers. We each had imaginary teams of eleven 'men' and took our games pretty seriously. John's side was virtually always the 'PFM', which stood for 'Percher Final Matches'. As if that were not strange enough, my team was always 'My Nice Mouses'. John had Nice Mouses too but his never played cricket. I'm not sure if I ever won, any more than I could defeat my older brother in a straightforward fight, though I must have tried pretty hard and often. It wasn't till I was sixteen that I overtook him in height and weight; and by then we no longer wanted to fight.

On the south side of the house we could play in the morning but not in the afternoon, which was sacred to mama's rest time. She took to her bed from 2 to 4 p.m. every day. Immediately below her windows was the terrace, which was gravelled, with flowerbeds next to the house and a grass edge and bank on the opposite side. At the far end, beyond the greenhouse, was a steep little path that led via an archway in a wall to the vegetable garden. We used to roll balls down this hill and see whose could get furthest. This game was one constituent of what was later to become a major family preoccupation – the 'Pingway'. The other element from which that was to derive was a game we played with billiard cues and balls, using the cues in pairs as railway tracks and making the balls act as 'trains'. It was possible to make points and junctions and, with the aid of books to prop up the cues at various heights, quite a reasonable layout was attained.

The third and largest part of the garden consisted of the backyard with its numerous outbuildings, the chicken run, the pig sties and the vegetable garden, which itself was divided into three main parts separated by ash paths bordered by neat little box hedges, which never seemed to get any bigger. We used the vegetable garden as well as whatever else was at the time within bounds for games of hide and seek, favourite hiding places being beyond the soft fruit bushes at the bottom of the garden and in the asparagus beds. In all our time at Cuddesdon I don't remember asparagus ever being eaten. I certainly never had any myself but in the summer holidays its ferny foliage made a super hide.

None of us went to the village school. Indeed we were strongly discouraged from fraternising with the village boys, who doubtless would have taught us wicked ways and terrible accents. Mama was well qualified to teach us and ran a little school of her own in our dining room. Before her marriage she had taught at the Godolphin School in Salisbury.

When we were eight each of us boys in turn began life at the Manor House, Horsham, a prep school in Sussex commended to my parents by some cousins who already had a son there. If one had to go away to a boarding school, I don't suppose they could have chosen better. Certainly my memories of my time there were nearly all happy ones. The first that was not concerned the death of grampapha.

On a visit to his home in Trentham, where he was vicar as well as being Archdeacon of Stoke, we were warned by Papa to be very careful not to damage the water lilies which were my grandfather's pride and joy. There were three or four lily ponds. One day I fell into one of them and broke not one but some five or six of his lilies. I was of course very wet and slightly bruised as a result of my tumble but my one concern was that I was about to be murdered by grampapha. In the event he was kindness itself, much more concerned by my supposed nearly drowning than about his broken lilies. So I was greatly relieved. For some strange reason however I was still somewhat afraid of him, which is why I was surprised at the extent of my grief when, during my first term at the Manor House, the headmaster broke the news of his death to John and me. I wept buckets at a time when crying was taboo. Looking back on this I guess my real chief cause of grief was my separation from home and family, but that of course couldn't possibly be admitted even into my own consciousness.

I was reasonably good at games and highly successful academically, which in those days counted for much more than it did later. I was expected to gain a scholarship to some public school and in due course both John and I fulfilled these expectations, he gaining top scholarship and I third place, both at St Edward's, Oxford.

The most difficult experience I had to deal with while at Horsham was the homosexual attentions I received from two of my teachers. Neither of them did me any harm that I know of. Both were undoubtedly genuinely fond of me. What went through their minds I cannot say but they never went further physically than giving me passionate hugs in dark corners just before I went upstairs to bed.

In the summer term after my eleventh birthday the Vicar of Horsham prepared me for confirmation. I remember just two things about the classes: we all liked him and he gave us each a sweet every time we met. One day shortly before the confirmation I stood outside the school chapel and had an important little conversation with myself. 'When people grow up', I said, 'they mostly seem to abandon their religion as if it were something for children only. At this moment I am absolutely certain about God and his love for me and of the basic truths of the Christian faith. I suppose I shall be tempted to give up like other people do. If I am so tempted may I remember this moment of total certainty. I don't believe that adults are any wiser than children. What I know to be true now will always be true, no matter how I feel.' Fairly often I've needed to remember that moment and the decision I made then has served me well.

I suppose my mother had given me *some* sex education but nothing that lodged in my mind. At school there was nothing officially done about this but obviously we learned a thing or two in unplanned ways. I remember being horribly embarrassed by my first unwanted erections, which I didn't know how to hide. The secret pleasures of masturbation were imparted to me by a fellow pupil who slept in the bed next to mine. Everything to do with sex seems to have been guilt inducing. This was made worse when my father, in the summer holidays after I left the Manor House, had a shot at teaching me the facts of life I needed to know before going on to St Edward's. He took ages to explain what I knew already, ensuring that I understood masturbation to be sinful and fornication, adultery or any other sexual coupling outside of marriage to be almost on a par with murder in the hierarchy of wickedness. The only slight relief in all this was that he did talk briefly about wet dreams, which were not to be classed as sins. That was a slight relief because I certainly had felt guilty about them.

CHAPTER III

Shortly before I went to St Edwards the newspapers published details of the latest single-engined fighter plane that was shortly to come into service with the RAF. I was absolutely smitten by it. I'd taken no notice of the advent of the Hawker Hurricane, which had marked a great advance on the old Gloster Gladiator, a biplane with which all our fighter squadrons had been equipped when I'd first felt any interest in flying. Now came the Spitfire; and here was I, aged thirteen, determined that one day I would be a Spitfire pilot.

By this time my mother's childbearing had finished and I had two more siblings – Elisabeth and Martin. In later years Martin let his siblings know that he felt we gave him a rough time and that his childhood was a miserable one. My recollections don't bear that out. Elisabeth certainly did have a rough time, largely because of her dyslexia – a not understood and undiagnosed condition in those days and other troubles with her eyes; nor did it help her when my parents 'adopted' Ingrid. She came to us from a German family. Her maternal grandmother was a Jewess and her parents very wisely didn't want her to be brought up in Hitler's Germany. She was just a bit younger than Elisabeth and spoke barely a word of English when she came to us. Even my speaking to her in my rather elementary German did little to lessen her loneliness; but I soon felt she was a real member of the family. To me, she has been a sister ever since.

In school holidays Mama used to take some of us shopping in Oxford and when I went with her we nearly always had a rendezvous with Granny Buckle at 11 a.m. in the Cadena Café. Sometimes it was just Granny and I having our elevenses together while Mama did more shopping. I loved the smell of roasting and grinding coffee that wafted out from the front of the Cadena, no doubt designed to draw customers in. Granny used to have her own table and sat facing the entrance, gently inclining her formidable head towards anyone who came in, whom she knew and respected. I have a hunch that she studiously ignored a few whom she knew but did not respect.

She often talked to me about her noble son Garry who had been a colonel and was killed towards the end of the First World War. She spoke sometimes too about her gallant military brothers, who were clearly heroes too. Strangely she didn't ascribe any heroism to her husband in spite of the fact that he had risen to be a General and had won a CB, CMG and DSO. While they lived at Iffley, Granhardy market gardened. He inspired me with a love of gardening and at a later stage in my life I for a short time followed in his footsteps in a minor way. Granny never referred to him as 'my husband' but always as 'the General'. His immediate forefathers had been admirals and their pictures adorned the walls of their dining room. Granny used to imply that any male descendant of theirs was expected to put on the King's uniform and if possible die for his country.

I'd been Captain of the School (Head Boy) at the Manor House; so the change to being a new boy at Teddy's meant coming down to earth with a bump. My brother John was there already and had explained some of the odd customs we were expected to master within a day or two of arrival. I was one of three new boys in our house – Apsley, which was presided over by a plump and kindly bachelor, J.F.W. Eardley. The head of house was twenty when he finally left school and the senior prefect had his twenty-first birthday in his last term, by which time he was also head of a local family firm of ironmongers.

A lesson we soon learned was that senior boys were a lot more important than junior masters. Prefects could punish their juniors with anything from the odd chore to a beating. The only masters who went that far were the housemasters and the warden (headmaster), whose beatings were rare events. For our first two years we spent our spare time in the junior dayroom, where three of the walls were supplied with 'horseboxes' – small cubicles with a writing surface and shelves in front of a wooden seat with a high back. In all there were some eighteen of these. Junior boys sat at desks just like those I'd been used to in my last three years at Horsham.

You might think we'd have a lot of spare time but in fact there was very little: we were kept on the go from rising till bedtime. The rising bell was followed by a stampede to the bathroom, where we had a cold shower every morning. Then as soon as we'd hurriedly dressed we all trooped into chapel for morning prayers, conducted by one of the two school chaplains or the warden, who was also in holy orders. Breakfast was in the school dining hall but before the meal we went to our dayrooms for a half-hour of 'prep'. By 9 a.m. we were in our classrooms for the first two lessons of the day.

There was a break from 10.50 to 11.10. 'Ah!', you might think, 'A bit of relaxing now'. Not a bit of it. Within this break we had ten minutes of 'drill', conducted by Sergeant-Major Merry, a smart little man who cut the hair of every boy in the school, also doing his sergeant-majoring in the Officers Training Corps (OTC). He was deservedly popular and kept us well entertained with a limitless supply of stories while he was cutting hair. This drill was chiefly physical training and quite enjoyable but it didn't leave us enough spare time to do anything much.

Two more lesson periods took us to 12.55, after which we'd just time to get books back to the dayroom and get to the dining hall for lunch. The food was reasonably good though not up to the standard I was used to at home or at prep school. There followed a brief digestive pause before we would be off again, this time to the changing rooms to prepare for whichever sport was currently being pursued. In the winter term it was always rugger and this continued for the first part of the Easter term, which however ended with hockey and athletics. In the summer term there was a choice between cricket and rowing. Then on one day a week we had 'corps' (the OTC), when we all had to pretend to be soldiers and were drilled and marched around the playing fields, occasionally being taught more exciting things such as how to assemble and disassemble a Lee-Enfield rifle or even a Bren gun.

I quite enjoyed this military activity, especially the annual camp, when we'd be taken off to some distant military establishment and live under canvas and generally do the sort of things we've all become familiar with when watching *Dad's Army* on television. After two years in the corps one was free to opt out of army training and transfer to the Sea Cadets or the Air Training Corps (ATC). Naturally I took the second option and so began in a small way my preparation to become a Spitfire pilot.

In the summer term cricket and rowing came after tea with lessons in the afternoon. In the other two terms tea was followed by the classroom periods. Always evening chapel came just before supper, which was followed by an hour and a quarter's prep in our dayrooms; then bed for juniors and for seniors a short break followed by another half-hour of prep. Prep was supervised by one of the house prefects who had to get their own work done while ensuring there was no misbehaviour by his charges, who had to keep strict silence and get the prefect's permission to leave the room or do anything other than sit and work.

Our sleeping accommodation was primitive. The head of house had his own bedroom. The rest of us slept in two vast dormitories, one for the junior dayroom and the other for the prefects and the senior dayroom. We were rationed to one blanket apiece and all the windows were always open at night. Occasionally I felt on the cold side but that wasn't ever a serious problem.

Even with an older brother in my house I failed to understand why some things went the way they did. Like other new boys I always half expected to be punished for infringing some rule or custom I'd not yet mastered. On one occasion a small boy was given a punishment that was so horrific that I could only assume he'd committed some absolutely unpardonable offence. The cry went up, 'Arse-hole him.' He was then made to stand in the wooden waste paper bin with his face to the wall. He was debagged and one after another of the older boys plunged their forearms into the waiting anus of the victim who of course kept his mouth firmly shut.

In later life when I had a bit of prostate trouble, the gentle probing by the doctor with gloved hand brought that poor boy's ordeal back to me. I was somewhat sensitive in the anal area anyway, being prone to constipation and developing piles at the age of fourteen, which were to trouble me on and off for most of my life. I don't recall receiving any treatment for this trouble until after the war, so I suppose it couldn't have been very severe.

While at Teddy's I did have two nasty bits of health trouble. First I got mumps. In those days most children did and there's not that much to it: a swollen and aching jaw and that's soon over. The difference in my case was that I got orchitis – inflammation of the testicles, which swelled like balloons and made the aching jaw seem trivial indeed. During this illness I was in the San (sanatorium), the school's own little hospital, for about a month and felt very sorry for myself; all the more so when a careless nurse, giving me a blanket bath, crashed her hand into my most vulnerable spot, causing me to raise the roof with my shout of pain. Alas, I'm not good at silent endurance.

The other bit of trouble occurred when I fell over on our slippery bathroom floor and landed on my left elbow. The pain was extreme and the following morning the whole of my upper arm had gone blue-black. Our house matron rubbed it with some soothing ointment but, though the brilliant colours gradually faded, the arm was still very uncomfortable. Finally I was sent into the town to a masseur, who of course massaged it. He was very gentle but the pain was still unpleasant and I didn't go back for more. By this time the school doctor had decided that I'd had quite enough treatment and took me off the sick list, so that the next day I was playing rugger again. The first time I was tackled I fell on my left arm, which was clearly not OK. This time I was X-rayed. The result showed that my humerus was broken from elbow to shoulder, had reset itself crookedly and was now broken again. After that my arm was fixed to my trunk with elastoplast and I had to learn to dress myself and even do up my shoe laces with the right hand only – a feat I could still accomplish until, in my seventies, arthritis made it too difficult.

Fagging was part of the public school system in those days. At the time it was completely taken for granted and I personally had no objection to it. The chief jobs we had to do as fags were to clean and polish shoes and rugger boots for our house prefects and to cook them bacon and eggs on a gas ring on Saturday afternoons. We ceased to be fags at the end of our first year. I took a pride in getting a high polish on shoes, which was to serve me in good stead in the early days of my RAF career.

CHAPTER IV

When commenting on the very small amount of free time we enjoyed, it might be thought that life at public school was a lot worse than I found it to be. Of course, there were unpleasant things but the reason for all the hyperactivity was obvious enough: it was to prevent sexual hanky-panky. I was glad to have escaped from the mild form of it I'd had at the Manor House. Now at Teddy's everyone was aware of what we called 'tarting'. Big boys formed relationships with attractive little boys, who were known as tarts, whether they liked it or not. Pairs would sneak off into nearby woodlands when there was enough time to do so. It was anyone's guess what then happened. For my part I suspect not very much – probably much the same stuff as I'd put up with at Horsham. Certainly no one boasted of a successful seduction.

For the vast majority of us any sexual satisfaction had to be solitary. In my case this left me with a constant semiconscious feeling of guilt, which was only dealt with when, at the age of fifteen, I had a long and most helpful talk with Michael Peck, then a curate at Greenford, who had been my favourite Cuddesdon Theological College student and who was a wonderful friend to the end of his life. He was very wise and incredibly good with youngsters. Whenever he walked around the streets he would be followed by hordes of kids, the younger ones often clinging to the cassock he always wore when about his work.

Michael was full of jokes and fun. Soon after his arrival in the parish he was invited to a social evening at the local Conservative club. After he'd accepted his rector warned him that they would try to make him drunk. Now Michael had been a medical student at Cambridge and knew a thing or two about how to cope with alcohol. Before setting out for the club he ate some charcoal dog biscuits, stuffing several more into his pockets. The party went with a swing and he kept pace with his hosts. Several times during the evening he retired to the gents and ate another biscuit. Gradually the party got somnolent. By midnight Michael was the only person still awake; so he wrote a note and left it on a table in the middle of the room.

It said: 'Thank you so much for a most enjoyable evening. When I left there didn't seem to be anyone I could say goodbye to.'

Michael used to get up a party of boys each Easter week to sail on the Norfolk Broads. I'd done some sailing in a thirty-ton Bristol Channel Pilot Cutter with Hallam McDiarmid and a crew of seven young men and boys when I was thirteen. In my fifteenth and sixteenth years I was in Michael's Broads party. We sailed from Acle with two boats, the *Syringa* and the *Moss Rose*. Christopher Stead skippered *Syringa* and Michael was Commodore and skipper of *Moss Rose*. My brother John was in the party too and he founded a society for those of us who went sailing together. He called it 'The Society for Anonymous Different Enterprises', or Spade Club for short. We had several burgees made with a King's, Cambridge purple spade on a white background. All boats sailing with us flew this burgee. Later Michael changed our name to 'The Society for Any Damned Enterprise'. When war came, sailing on the Broads was out but other ways of holidaying together came in.

Sailing on the Broads was adventure enough for me at the time. We used to write up the log of the day's events and read them aloud each evening. Each boat had its own logographer and I wrote one of them on my second trip. Sailing on *Queen* with Hallam and company in the holidays between leaving the Manor House and going to St Edward's was a much more hairy affair. The weather had been awful for the first half of the fortnight we had together. We stayed anchored in Milford Haven for the first two days after coming downstream from our moorings at Lawrenny. Then, in spite of gale warnings we ventured out into the Irish Sea and were soon up against it. I became so seasick that I lost all interest in the problems we faced but learned in due course that we had come as near as possible to getting wrecked just inshore from a lighthouse. It was only in our second week that I was able to be of any use as a crewmember. I remember the wonderful feeling I had when alone at the helm at night, sailing in a gentle breeze, in sole command for a short time of this great ship (as she seemed to me) with all seven of the other people asleep below.

Eventually, having visited but not anchored off the east and south coasts of Ireland, and going a little way out into the wide Atlantic, we returned to Milford Haven. While at anchor in the harbour I heard a meowing and said to Hallam, 'I'd like to go over to that cliff there and see if I can rescue that cat.'

'That's not a cat; it's a kittiwake gull,' was his reply, 'but you can take the dinghy and have a look if you like.' Which I did. Pulling it ashore at the foot of the cliff I was able to leave the dinghy in safety and climb towards the still meowing 'kittiwake'. The ascent took me about ten minutes of not very difficult climbing. To my joy I found that it really was a kitten, perched on a narrow ledge and certainly needing to be rescued. I collected her and brought her back to *Queen*. I called her 'Kittywake' and she stayed with me till her untimely death by drowning some three years later.

She was an extraordinary cat, for nor only did she insist on leaping off the boat into the sea, a drop of nine feet, but also she regularly swam around her and then clambered up the anchor chain. When I got her home she followed me, like a dog, wherever I went, including long walks around Cuddesdon and even jumping into the river and swimming with me. Though she'd not been able to get off that ledge on the cliff side by herself, she seemed capable of almost anything when in my company. On the last day of her life Kittiwake came swimming with us in the River Thame. While in the water she had what looked like an epileptic fit. When I finally fished her out she was dead. I was devastated by her loss and carried her home and gave her a solemn burial in the shrubbery that bordered the vicarage drive.

At school I was academically as successful to begin with as I'd been at the Manor House. Indeed my French was so far superior to that of anyone else in the class that I found it deadly boring. I continued to shine at maths and took up German. Towards the end of my first summer term we sat for the School Certificate exam, which I passed with seven credits. Next term I was in the Modern Languages Sixth Form at the tender age of fourteen. Two years later I passed the Higher Certificate Exam with Distinctions in French and German. The only sad thing about all this was that I had to give up maths. I regret having had to specialise at such an early age but, since I had to, my choice of languages was one I did not regret.

The outbreak of war had an immediate impact on Teddy's in several ways. The most significant from my point of view was that my form master and a good many other members of staff rushed off to join the army. This meant that a number of barely qualified teachers took their places. The Modern Languages Sixth was taken over by one Reginald Maxse. He was in his late seventies when he joined us and he stayed at his post right through the war. He was a fascinating man, having been private tutor to the family of the last Tsar of Russia and also to the last Emperor of Austro-Hungary. As if that were not enough he'd also been a spy for Britain, based in

Switzerland, during the First World War. He claimed to be fluent in every European language but his English accent was very continental. My hopes of winning a scholarship to Cambridge collapsed pretty well completely after I'd experienced a term or two of his teaching. The main trouble was that he so easily got side-tracked into telling us stories about his life that little real work got done. In September 1940 I sat for my scholarship and came fourth last out of 126 candidates. However it was enough for me to secure a place at King's, where I had many connections including my brother John who had succeeded in gaining a scholarship in Classics.

When I knew what lay in store for me if I survived the war I decided to join the RAF as soon as possible and to enjoy my last two terms by not bothering at all about my academic progress. I was given lots of spare time for what were known as 'study periods', which were spent in the school library in a cosy corner, playing bridge with like-minded boys. I also organised the occasional sherry party, which would not have gone down well had I been discovered by my housemaster.

In the autumn of 1940 I was made editor of the St Edward's School *Chronicle*, a job I enjoyed enormously. I had plenty of time to go round persuading boys to write poems or prose contributions and to collect the various stories about our sporting achievements, which were always chronicled by the appropriate members of staff. The specially pleasant thing about the job was that it entitled me to free copies of the *Chronicle* for the rest of my life. Though I'm not now a great supporter of the public school system, I am at least able to get a true picture of what life at Teddy's is like today and have to admit that what they do there is very impressive. The financial side is staggering. While John, Stephen and I were there the fees at Teddy's were pretty static at around £127 a year. John's £100 scholarship meant that he only cost my parents £9 a term, while I with my £70 scholarship cost them £19. Stephen with a clergy bursary was much the most expensive. Fees for him were £29 a term. My guess is that this outlay was less than we would have cost had we stayed at home. I've not asked what the present fees are but know that even the top scholarship wouldn't bring the bill down below several thousand pounds a year.

Teddy's was a very churchy school and in my book that was a very good thing. The main advantage was that all major Saints' days were observed with half-holidays. We had chapel services twice a day and an early Communion service for any who wanted to go. On Sundays we were free from after the 10 a.m. service until the Evening service at 6.30. If we went outside the school grounds we were supposed to wear our straw hats known as 'bashers'. This rule did not apply on the one occasion each term when we had an *exeat* (permission to go out). I could have been at home in Cuddesdon for much of this time but actually I very seldom made it. My parents would come perhaps once a year and occasionally I did the journey by bicycle, which took me around an hour each way.

During my last two years I started having a whale of a time in my personal spiritual life. Whatever the weather, as soon as lights were out in the senior dormitory and we had all settled down, I would get out of bed and down on my knees and in next to no time would be mentally and emotionally transported into another world. I had fallen in love with God in a big way. For quite a number of years I could get into a sort of trance-like state in which I felt perfectly warm and comfortable whatever the temperature might be – and sometimes it was really cold. What went on in chapel was all right but not significant for me. What went on in my private prayers was the most important thing in my life. I suppose all this had something to do with the priesthood I took up many years later; but at the time and for the next ten years I used to swear that whatever I did in life I'd never be a 'bloody parson'.

CHAPTER V

Back at home the war made enormous changes to our life. The nine o'clock news now came to dominate the evening and I spent some time studying the various voices of the newsreaders so that I could mimic them. I got particularly good at being Frank Phillips and was once able to use that skill to good effect. As soon as I was seventeen I joined the LDV, which later became the Home Guard. The Cuddesdon contingent was tiny and I think I was the only one under sixty-five. We never did anything like as much as I'd already done in the school 'corps' but I do remember an occasion when we met a few bedraggled and miserable soldiers who'd just got back from Dunkirk. One of them told me in an unforgettable phrase: 'We didn't fucking want to fuck the fuckers.' When I finally got into the Air Force I was pleased to find that the language in use was more colourful and varied than that of the army.

Across the road from our house was the Bishop's Palace. This vast building had forty-two bedrooms and for some years had been occupied by a single man and his staff. He was Bishop Tommy Strong who was so scared of women that if one approached him in his house he was said to have hidden behind the curtains. He was good with young men and boys and John and I used to take him an Easter Egg every year until he retired. It was always decorated with a white icing piped inscription: 'My Lord'.

Soon after the war started the bishop moved to Oxford and his palace was occupied by a band of young women, clerks to Queen Anne's Bounty, a charity which helped finance the clergy of the Church of England. Hitherto Cuddesdon had had plenty of young men but young women were scarce. Now we had an abundance of available female company and I soon found myself getting involved with one of the younger ones over the road. Walking arm in arm in the Bishop's Wood by moonlight was as far as it ever got. My mother thought that was quite far enough and warned me one day that I was playing with fire and might hurt the young lady quite a lot though I might well not suffer at all myself. She was right. On reflection I decided quietly to drop her, which did cause a bit of pain to both of us but for me the expectation that I'd soon be in the Air Force was a bigger affair.

My chief holiday occupation was the creation of a telephone system. I began work on this when I was fifteen but by this time I'd become ambitious and had two subscribers a considerable distance from our house. The major problem was to get the wire I needed for this extended system. I made delicate enquiries from an official of the Post Office who lived locally. 'What', I asked, 'was going to happen to the two miles of telephone wires that ran beside the road down to the mill and on beyond?' I'd noticed that one small section had come down and clearly there was no hurry to repair it. My kindly informant told me that for the duration of the war nothing whatever would be done about it. It might, he thought, be taken down and scrapped one day but the GPO was frankly not interested. But I was. So, taking a length of rope, I used to go down that road two or three times a week and with my lasso and a pair of pliers would secure vast quantities of beautiful copper wire, which enabled me to do all the wiring I wanted for my own system.

The Sunday evening Bright Hour still took place in term time, but usually my father would insist on hearing at least the headlines of the nine o'clock news. It struck me that I could brighten up the proceedings with my two skills – telephone engineering and mimicry. So one Sunday in May 1940 I asked my father if he'd be sure to turn on the news at nine. He agreed, knowing that I was up to something but not what that something was.

Our drawing room was packed and we had a distinguished clerical visitor. At nine the radio was switched on and the voice of 'Frank Phillips' announced that German parachute troops had landed near Oxford and a vast armada of enemy aircraft was attacking. Heavy losses had already been inflicted on the invading forces. And now the Prime Minister would address the nation. Then 'Mr Churchill' made a powerful speech, incorporating most of the phrases I'd learned from listening to his previous efforts. After which a big bang was organised. Then 'Frank Phillips' was back on the air to say that the Prime Minister had been killed when his underground shelter at 10 Downing Street had been demolished by the direct hit of a German bomb. Further news was given, ending with the announcement that German forces were approaching the small village of Cuddesdon, which was of no strategic importance. At this point I left my microphone and came downstairs to join the party. Nearly everyone was laughing heartily but the distinguished visitor was repeating again and again, 'There's no need to get hysterical.'

CHAPTER VI

My eighteenth birthday fell on Good Friday; so the recruiting office was closed Next day I reported there and enlisted in the RAF, being accepted as a would-be flying cadet. To my surprise there seemed to be no urgency at all about getting me into uniform to start training. I was told to go away and wait to be called up.

I'd already left Teddy's, expecting to get straight into active service on my birthday or in the next day or two. So I had to decide how to fill in the time of waiting. I wrote to Harold Layton, Headmaster of Manor House, to ask if by any chance he could do with some help by me teaching there. He replied by return of post and said I'd be most welcome, for just as at Teddy's, the younger members of the teaching staff had all gone off to war. I thought there might be some difficulty between myself and my brother Stephen who was just beginning his final term as a Manor House pupil. In point of fact it all went very well and he never failed to call me 'Sir' in term time; indeed, he continued to do so well into the following summer holidays.

Although the war was going badly, that bothered me very little. I was supremely confident that we'd win through and was completely convinced by all our propaganda and the gross exaggerations of our brave boys' prowess by sea, land and air. I busied myself teaching maths and French and also playing cricket. I was a member of the Old Boys' team that played the school First XI, of which my brother Stephen was a distinguished member. He had the misfortune to be hit painfully on the foot by one of my better straight yorkers. I and the keeper both appealed vociferously. Stephen hobbled about for some time in obvious pain and then indicated that he was ready to go on with his innings, only to discover that he had been given out lbw. He very generously never held it against me.

In mid-August I joined a Spade Club expedition walking in the Lake District and was lucky enough to have almost a week there before the summons came from the RAF. Each day we tended to walk a bit further than the last and to cover as many peaks as we could fit in. On my last day with the party we climbed both Skiddaw and Saddleback and walked thirty miles in the process. Then came the phone call from home telling me that the summons had come from the Air Force to report at Lord's cricket ground in London in two days' time. That was the end of a great holiday, which had incidentally got me very fit and ready for service.

Lord's was a gloomy place at that time and it was raining when I reported there along with some two hundred others. We collected our uniforms, checked that they fitted and were then marched in very unservice-like fashion to our billets, which were flats in St John's Wood. In addition to the uniform we were issued with a hussif (housewife), which had the wherewithal to do a bit of sewing and darning, and some shoe cleaning equipment, the two brushes of which are still being used today sixty years after they were issued to me.

The billets were not comfortably equipped, consisting of rooms with bare boards and straw palliasses the only furniture. However we did have hot and cold water and a bath could be taken. We ate our meals in London Zoo close by, whither we were marched in a somewhat smarter manner than we'd used on our first arrival. There was nothing wrong with the food but we were all anxious to get away from the billets and the zoo and to get started on proper training. During the week we spent in London we had a few talks from different officers on various subjects which were supposed to be of interest to us. The only one I recall at all was a stupid harangue by a 'penguin' (a non-flying RAF officer) in which he informed us that our job was to hate, hate, hate the Germans and remember that the only good Germans were dead ones. I don't recall ever meeting any pilot who went along with that xenophobic rubbish and had very good cause later on to know what nonsense it was.

Those of us who shared a room and a good many more of us were posted to the Initial Training Wing at Scarborough in Yorkshire – No.11 ITW. We were billeted in a hotel facing the South bay. But for the fact that the hotel had received a German bomb the previous night it would have been a great improvement on our London billets. As it was we found our new home had no glass in the windows, no hot water and no electricity. The food was OK but inadequate in quantity and we soon found that it was more or less essential to supplement our diet from the various canteens in the town manned by volunteers. We were paid once a week the princely sum of half a crown a day, of which I always spent a shilling on food. I smoked in moderation but still managed to save sixpence a day, thus starting the habit of always putting something by, however straitened my circumstances.

The purpose of the ITW was to instil into us service discipline and to give us a grounding in those academic subjects which were vital if we were to become pilots or navigators. We did lots of drill, being marched up and down by a fierce Flight Sergeant McTaggart, who was determined that we were to become the smartest unit in the RAF. One of his favourite expressions was 'Bullshit baffles brains.'

When I first heard this phrase I hadn't a clue as to its meaning. When dissatisfied with our performance he would shout out 'By Jesus Christ I'll have your guts for garters!' This I *was* able to translate; it simply meant 'Smarten up or you'll smart for it.' The first meaning of 'bullshit', I learned, was spit and polish and general smartness on parade. The more widely used sense of 'rubbish' was not one I recall being used in those days.

On the academic front I found the classes pretty boring as I'd covered most of the ground while in the ATC at Teddy's. After the first week they changed my status from pupil to instructor for the classes in mathematics. This at least made it more interesting for me. In fact I got quite a kick out of my teaching role.

We had a reasonable amount of spare time and one of the first things I did was to pay a call on the home of the Vicar of Scarborough in order to find out where his curate, David Dewing, lived. David had been a friend in his student days at Cuddesdon and I was anxious to have some ties locally outside the RAF. I got more and much better than I bargained for. When I was met at the door by Mrs Patteson and had explained who I was and what I wanted she invited me to come in and have tea with the family. Tea was had in the drawing room at the top of the house but was made far below on the ground floor or possibly even in the basement kitchen. When the time came to pour out, there came forth only water. This got us off to a splendid start with ice thoroughly broken. The big thrill was meeting Sylvia, the second daughter, then fifteen and stunningly beautiful. I was sure I would be back on some pretext before long. The attraction was mutual but it was to be a long time before it was acknowledged.

In October we were posted to a transit camp at Padgate, near Warrington. Then came the Atlantic crossing from Liverpool to Halifax, Nova Scotia, in Canada. The voyage was memorable for several reasons: first I was allotted a 'berth' on F deck at the very bottom of the ship, which was the *SS Pasteur*, known by everyone as the 'Past 'er best'. She was a French liner built to capture the Blue Riband of the Atlantic and completed just before the outbreak of war. The Royal Navy had taken her off the French when France capitulated and she'd been converted into a troopship, There were five thousand of us on board and down on F deck we were packed in like sardines. I slept on the floor; someone else on a table above me and a third person in a hammock slung above the table. On the second day out I developed nettle-rash, which made my life a misery throughout the voyage, which was mercifully short since the *Pasteur* was indeed a fast ship and made the crossing in five days.

We reckoned we must be terribly important people, for as we set sail a fleet of Royal Navy ships joined us: an aircraft-carrier, a cruiser and five destroyers. On the second day out they all left us except for two destroyers. We gathered that the rest were headed for the Mediterranean. On the third day there was enormous excitement as our escorts began dashing around dropping depth charges. One of the destroyers went a long way off but returned to signal triumphantly some such words as 'Sighted Sub. Sank same'. Between them they reckoned to have destroyed two U-boats, for which we were properly grateful.

CHAPTER VII

I was strangely glad to find it very cold when we disembarked at Halifax. In next to no time my nettle-rash disappeared. We went by train to Moncton, New Brunswick, where we got our first real taste of Canada and the hospitality of its citizens. Moncton for us was another transit camp. From there we were due to go off to many different places for our flying training, some staying in Canada and others going down to the USA.

I have two abiding memories of that first visit to Moncton. First there was an amazing hospitality. I walked down a street and the first person I met said 'Come home with me and meet the family and have a meal with us.' Just like that! And I did just that and was persuaded to spend much of my spare time with that family. The other memory is of the snow. The day we arrived there was a light dusting everywhere. Then it snowed all night and into the day following. When we left our billets it was to walk down a corridor about four feet wide with walls of snow on either side, rising to some six feet in height. The speed with which snow got cleared still astonishes me when I think about it and compare it with what happens now in Britain, when it always seems to catch us unprepared.

We had five or six days at Moncton and were then put on board a train in which we travelled for three days and two nights, being served the most amazing meals, with specially printed menus provided and *choices* among a whole series of delicious alternatives. Back home by this stage in the war food rationing was severe and though we fared better than civilians we'd not seen food like this since before the war. Indeed, as far as I was concerned, I'd hardly ever been treated to such feasts as we enjoyed on that journey.

Our destination was Montgomery, Alabama, where we arrived early in November. We'd moved from a near arctic climate to the warm Deep South of America. We were housed in very comfortable barracks with stoeps (verandas) running down their South fronts. This was the start of our relationship with the US Army Air Corps, to which we were to be attached for the rest of our time in America.

The basic purpose of our short stay at Montgomery was to acclimatise us to US Army conditions and their air corps language. We learned for instance that aeroplanes were 'ships' and that junior officers were 'lootenants' though spelt the same way as our 'leftenants' (lieutenants). We marvelled at the sloppy way our American army friends marched around as casually as if they were out with their girlfriends. By contrast we demonstrated the kind of bullshit so strongly instilled into us by F/Sgt McTaggart back at ITW and reckoned we were about as smart as the Brigade of Guards.

We had a lot of spare time and again found the local population amazingly hospitable. I quickly discovered the Episcopal Church and repaired there on my first Sunday. It was another astonishing experience. The service itself was not too different from what I was used to, except that there was no sermon and the collection quite bowled me over. As I entered the church I was confronted with two enormous wooden bowls already piled high with notes – ten, twenty-five, fifty and hundred dollar bills. If there were any coins there they were simply placed so as to stop the paper from blowing away.

After the Blessing which concluded the service – or so I thought – the whole congregation moved into the hall adjoining and settled down in extremely comfortable chairs. Many people collected drinks, mostly alcoholic; and many people lit up – mostly cigars. After some ten minutes of chat, when I was warmly welcomed by the Rector and others, we all became quiet and heard the sermon, delivered from a stage at one end of the hall by the Revd Edgar Ralph Neff, the Rector. He was a huge man in every way and appeared genuinely thrilled to meet one of the RAF boys. We were the first lot to descend on Montgomery, to be followed over the next few years by many others.

The next morning I was exploring the town when I saw Mr Neff approaching me. He hailed me from afar and said 'Hi there, Peter. Come into the drug store and have some elevenses with me.' In we went and without any consultation with me he said to the young lady behind the counter, 'Hi Miss. We'll have two large T-bone steaks and two coffees.' That, I thought, is not what I'd expect for elevenses but my thoughts were far short of guessing the reality. When the steaks appeared I'd never seen anything remotely like them, even in films. The plates were as big as any dinner plate one could imagine and they were completely covered by one-inch-thick beefsteaks. What I'd got in front of me was, I thought, about a year's meat ration at home. I did sample it and it was beautifully tender and quite delicious. I could even see how someone of my companion's size could cope with it; but it was far beyond me, who had already had a sizeable cooked breakfast only some two and a half hours earlier.

In the local paper I was amused to read an account of our marching through the town when we'd first arrived in Montgomery. There was a big picture of us marching in our highly disciplined fashion, while the accompanying article described the onlookers as shivering in the first autumn chill. To us it seemed like a very warm summer day.

It was while we were here that the Japanese attack on Pearl Harbour occurred. This greatly changed many things. Most obviously it meant that America was now in the war with us, not merely cheering us on from the sidelines. Of course the help we'd had from them was already of vital importance, as the fact that we were being trained to fly by the US Army Air Corps amply demonstrated. Flying training for the RAF had already spread around the British Empire, many pilots and navigators learning their stuff in Canada or Rhodesia. But we were the first bunch to be actually trained by the USA. There was of course some flying training done in Britain but the weather conditions were so much more favourable in other parts of the world and the absence of any chance attack by enemy aircraft meant that a far better and quicker job could be done by this dispersed method.

I much admired my own flying instructor whose name was Bartlebaugh. He belonged to an archery club and described how he spent his vacations hunting boar and stag with his deadly arrows. He must have been at least fifty but was young in heart and very experienced. He'd once flown under a local river bridge which he showed me. My guess was that the aircraft going through it would have had a clearance of about six inches on each side and only a few feet above and below.

I did my first flight with him on 20 December and that was the first time I'd ever been aloft. It was a big thrill and, though we were only up for fifteen minutes on that first trip, I had the chance to feel what it was like to control the aircraft. It was not easy at first even to keep flying straight and level. As for taking off and landing that had to wait for another day. The aircraft we flew was the Stearman PT 17, a biplane with a powerful 220 hp engine, a much larger and more robust aeroplane than the Tiger Moth which was the universally used primary trainer in the RAF.

After a dozen trips of instruction, Mr Bartlebaugh climbed out and said 'Now you're on your own. Just take off and get used to the feel of it and land again in quarter of an hour's time.' That first solo was another thrilling landmark. By now the most difficult thing was landing. We were supposed always to land on three points simultaneously – the two wheels and the tail skid. This manoeuvre was accomplished by stalling the plane at the precise moment, ideally about an inch above the ground. Because it was difficult we spent quite a lot of time doing what was called 'circuits and bumps', just taking off, circling the field and landing again.

CHAPTER VIII

As in Montgomery, I quickly found my way to the Episcopal Church in Tuscaloosa, which was rather more like what I'd been used to at home. The Rector was Richard Watson and he was as warmly welcoming as Mr Neff had been. He was slimmer and his hospitality was actually rather more to my taste. He used to entertain a dozen or so students from the local university and it was at a gathering of them that I met Betty Jones. She was a Methodist and her father was a millionaire. Their home was at Daytona Beach, Florida, where Betty kept her own private yacht. This was not the sort of boat I'd sailed on the Norfolk Broads but a craft of some one hundred tons with her own captain and crew. When we got to know each other better she invited me to come for a cruise but I never did it, probably out of cowardice, for I was afraid of getting entangled deeper than I meant to.

On Christmas Eve there was a national panic which both annoyed and amused us. The rumour was that we were about to be invaded by the Japanese; though why that should have caused such concern in Alabama was a puzzle to everyone. All military personnel were confined to barracks; and that included us. Twenty-four hours later on Christmas morning the ban on going out was still in force though no work of any kind was to be done on Christmas Day. I did a bit of research and found seven or eight men who were willing to come with me to a Communion service if we could get to the church. I then went through all the proper channels and eventually got to the Station Commander who gave us permission to be absent from camp for two hours in order to indulge in Christmas worship.

The next thing of course was to ring Mr Watson to see what, if anything, was still on at his church. The poor man had just got home for his Christmas dinner with his family. It was midday and he had already presided at four Communion services. Without a moment's hesitation he said, 'Come down as soon as you can and I'll be in church waiting for you.' So we got our service and even managed to sing a carol before we let the poor Rector get home to his family. We ourselves got back in time for a late lunch; our big meal being in the evening.

With the fairly recent experience of being an editor behind me I undertook to edit the station's magazine, which we called 'Fins and Flippers'. I was fortunate in finding a good photographer and the main feature was an illustrated mini-biography of everyone on the station. We had a splendid cover picture of one of our trainee pilots sitting astride a Stearman facing the tailplane, in which position he had actually done a circuit and landing, through the skill of his instructor who had accidentally ejected him from the cockpit owing to the slight oversight, by which his safety harness had remained unfixed.

I completed my primary flying training in February 1942 and we then moved on to our first real US Army base at Gunter Field, which was back on the outskirts of Montgomery. Here we were to do our basic military flying training, which was done on the Vultee BT13 aircraft, a low-winged monoplane, similar in its main characteristics to all contemporary fighter aircraft. Primary training had included aerobatics as well as all the essential things we needed to know in order to get around the sky by daylight. Now we learned how to fly on instruments by night and by day, and how to fly in various types of formation with other aircraft.

I tried a bit of aerial photography while up on my own and was reasonably satisfied with the results at the time. Later on I considered them rubbish; but the camera was not a good one and I really hadn't a clue how I should have gone about doing this sort of thing. I'd done sixty hours of flying training at Tuscaloosa and now I completed a further seventy hours on the BT13 and was ready to move to the final stage of my flying training.

We had all our weekends free and I used to hitch-hike the hundred miles from Gunter Field to Tuscaloosa for the Saturday night. Various kindly couples put me up and I invariably managed to spend a fair bit of time with Betty. On one of these occasions she suggested that we play golf, a game at which I was a total novice. All went reasonably well with me borrowing a spare set of clubs from her. That is to say until we got to the third tee. From that point the fairway led straight across a small lake, no more than twenty-five yards wide and situated only a hundred yards from the tee and well below it. 'Even I can clear that', I said to myself and proceeded to drive six balls in succession straight into the middle of the lake. I vowed then never to play golf again: a vow which I've more or less kept. I can't remember how we finished off that awful game, but Betty seemed to take it all very well and it did nothing to mar our friendship. This friendship was – outwardly at least – totally platonic, though towards the end of my time in America I sensed that she wasn't quite satisfied with that. Perhaps that invitation to cruise with her was something I did well to avoid, cowardly though it may have been. I did tell her one day that I had no intention of getting into a committed sexual relationship until the war was over; and neither of us wanted an uncommitted one.

My hosts in Tuscaloosa were invariably kind and considerate and made me feel very much at home. At first I had some difficulty getting used to the luxurious style of living, which was even superior to that which I'd known before the war. In spite of all the household gadgetry there were plenty of servants to wait on hosts and guests – all black of course – so that the householders never had to do any work in the home themselves.

As I look back now I am astonished that I so completely took for granted the total subordination of every black person to every white one. The only black people I met were servants. All were of the 'Uncle Tom' type, grateful to their wonderfully kind masters and mistresses for the way they were looked after. I remember being just a little surprised at their obsequiousness but not in the least shocked or upset. Racism was universal in the Deep South; and we all simply accepted it.

CHAPTER IX

Our next move was to Craig Field, Selma, still in Alabama and still within weekend range of Tuscaloosa. Here we did our Advanced Fighter Pilot training in the North American AT6, known over in England as the Harvard. It was a very noisy machine and its high-pitched hum was generally regarded as a bit of a pain by those on the ground hearing it. From the pilot's point of view the main snag was its very narrow undercarriage. Like the Spitfire the wheels moved outwards and upwards when they were retracted, whereas most undercarriages worked the other way, allowing the wheels to be much more widely spaced. I never heard of anyone groundlooping a Spitfire but the AT6 regularly suffered this punishment. You touched the brakes, which were controlled by pushing on the top of the rudder pedals. Push one of them a trifle too hard and the 'plane would do a violent U-turn and dig a wing-tip into the ground. This was a common but very unpopular trick and when I did it I feared that my pilot training might be brought to a sudden end. Fortunately I seem to have done fairly well in all other respects and not much was said about my mishap.

Part of our training at Selma was in night flying. The actual flying was a bit scary at first but I remember feeling great satisfaction at being able to land and take off and also to do some cross-country flying in the dark. The awful snag was that in the dormitory in which we slept there were only two of us doing night flying. While we did our best to sleep during the day, the rest of the cadets enjoyed the usual noisy behaviour of typical youngsters. I don't think I got any sleep at all between the two long nights we spent largely in the air and otherwise at work. I know I couldn't possibly have survived such an ordeal later in life.

Apart from the night flying most of what we learned at Craig Field was polishing up skills we already had begun to acquire: flying in various formations, flying high and using oxygen, flying on instruments only and navigating on cross-country flights. This last job was simple in the extreme by comparison with similar lessons we would later have in England. In Alabama in May and June there were no clouds in the sky and towns were so few and far between that you had to be really stupid to get lost. On top of all that there were radio beams to guide us should we by some remote chance run into clouds or mistake one town for another.

Early in June we moved to much more primitive surroundings at Eglin Field, Florida. Here we were on the coast of the Gulf of Mexico and slept under canvas. The heat was appalling and we were advised to wear gloves whenever we went about our duties, since to touch metal with bare hands meant serious burns. We were also told to be very wary of going for a swim in the Gulf. If we went in we should cover ourselves with towels until we actually entered the water and cover up again as soon as we got out. On no account were we to attempt sunbathing.

One day I risked a quick dip, carefully following all the instructions. To my amazement I saw lying on the beach no less a personage than my favourite film star, Lana Turner. I gawped briefly from a discrete distance out to sea. A fellow cadet who'd come in more or less with me spotted this vision of female beauty too and with immense courage and stupidity went straight up to her, placed his towel beside her on the beach and lay down and engaged her in conversation. I didn't wait to see how they got on for the heat really was most uncomfortable and I still can't imagine how the lady could bear it. The cadet certainly could not. Next day he was in hospital and some time later he was returned to England and discharged from the service as unfit. His burns were horrific. We all knew that we might one day have to face being burned through enemy action but nobody expected to get burned like that from a short spell of sunbathing.

We had red blankets on our beds but each time we entered our tent we'd find them black. Before climbing into bed we used to give the blanket a good shake to remove the cloud of flies which always settled on it when it was vacant. Having got into bed we would frequently be disturbed by rattlesnakes which seemed to enjoy brief tours of inspection of our humble abode. I'd no idea how lethal they were but mindful of Conan Doyle's Sherlock Holmes story called 'The Speckled Band' I had a horror of all snakes and never felt quite comfortable while we were in those tents.

Because of the extreme heat we used barely to eat except at breakfast which we ate in the cool of the early morning. That was a great meal. I used to start by eating a small packet of cereal and go on to consume ten eggs and twelve rashers of bacon, followed by several slices of toast with marmalade. Wherever we were stationed the food was always splendid both in quality and quantity. I'd weighed ten stone two pounds when I joined the RAF. When I returned from America I was a solid fourteen stone, a weight I maintained until I was shot down over France two years later.

At Eglin Field our main business was gunnery, shooting up targets on the ground and engaging in mock aerial combat with each other using cine-gun. We still did the occasional cross-country flight to keep up our navigational skills and it was on one of these flights that the whole unit got into a bit of trouble with a hurricane. We were all off in different areas when the hurricane arrived. As far as I recall we had absolutely no warning of its approach, which was sudden to put it mildly. I was trying to come in to land against a wind that was so strong that when heading into it I was actually moving backwards. The wind direction changed a bit and I began my descent virtually vertically with an airspeed of about 140 mph. I was about to congratulate myself on getting safely to earth when I suddenly found myself hurtling down the runway a few feet above ground at such a speed that putting down was clearly impossible. Climbing up again and thanking God I'd not touched down I attempted to return to the airfield which was now several miles behind me. The storm soon passed on its way and I think it must have been some ten minutes later that I got back to Eglin Field to find it relatively calm and landing quite simple. I'd been dead lucky for all the other aircraft of our unit that were airborne at the same time as I was had met greater or lesser disasters. The only one I remember clearly had landed very safely on a highway but had then been blown off the road and hit a wayside pole.

On 1 July I completed my Advanced Flying Training and was awarded our coveted wings. In the case of us RAF pilots we actually got two of these insignia, the ordinary ones of the RAF and the silver metal ones of the US Army Air Corps. Some of us were given commissions at the same time, while I with the majority of my compatriots was made a sergeant-pilot.

Two days after our Wings day we were crossing the border into Canada in the same sort of luxury train in which we'd come south eight months before. Back at Moncton, New Brunswick the atmosphere was completely changed for the worse. This was hardly surprising when we realised that literally thousands of RAF cadets had passed through the transit camp since our last visit. We were only here for a few days after which we boarded another train and headed for Halifax, laden with vast quantities of cigarettes and other goodies with which we hoped to bring cheer to our families when we got home.

I reckon I was very lucky to have had this opportunity to get to know a tiny bit of Canada and a bit more of America all at the expense of the government. Contrary to misguided expectations, I'd found the people I met were without exception friendly, kind and incredibly generous.

CHAPTER X

Our journey home from Halifax, Nova Scotia to Liverpool and Warrington was a great contrast to the outward one the previous autumn. Then there had been five thousand rookies. Now we were some one thousand trained pilots. We travelled fast, with two destroyers with us all the way and for some of the time we had air cover as well. This time I was very comfortably accommodated in a cabin instead of on the floor; and it was on B instead of F deck. I was loaded with goodies – more than a thousand cigarettes for myself, perfume and jewellery for my sisters and various other odds and ends which I cannot now remember. What I do remember vividly is the worry I and others had about the ordeal of going through customs on disembarking at Liverpool. Would I have the cash to pay? Would it have been better not to have brought such an enormous quantity of goods? None of us were prepared for what actually happened. Arrived at the customs checkpoint a smiling man stood there with a large piece of chalk with which he daubed a large cross on every piece of luggage we were manhandling in. As he did this he proclaimed loudly: 'RAF pilots have nothing to declare.'

We'd generally been very well treated by the American civilian population and now we discovered that wearing those coveted wings had a magical effect on people in England. Though it isn't the cowl that makes the monk and it isn't the uniform that makes the hero, it was startling to discover the enormous difference in the way I was treated when I was in that uniform as against my experiences when in mufti.

I had a fortnight's leave at home, finding we now lived in the Old Vicarage, the college having moved into our own house owing to the steep decline in numbers as students went off to join the forces. My older brother, John, who had been up at Cambridge when war broke out and had continued his studies for two years, was now also in the RAF and had gone out to Rhodesia to do his flying training there.

Our paths never crossed during our service careers, he becoming an Observer/Navigator on medium bombers, while I eventually progressed to my beloved Spitfires. But that was still some way off.

My next posting was to No. 17 (P)AFU, which I think stood for (Pilot) Aircraft Familiarisation Unit. I arrived with some fifteen others at Bodney, near Watton in Norfolk on the 24 August to begin flying in England. This was very different from flying in the USA. For a start the aeroplane was a Miles Master in place of the North American AT6. Then there was the weather. Over there the sun always shone. I suppose there must have been the odd cloud around now and then but we never flew in cloud. The only instrument flying was done at night after lots of practice in the Link trainer. Here the weather was a major factor. There we could navigate by radio beams even if it were not possible to spot the odd city up to one hundred miles away. Here you might be able to map read your way around the country but there was always the chance that the clouds would descend and force you to hedge hop or get up into the clouds and rely on instrument flying, which was not funny in those days. In theory you could navigate by dead reckoning but you still had to keep above any possible obstacles like high hills or the odd beacon and sooner or later you had to come down to earth – not much fun unless you were lucky enough to find a good break in the clouds at about the right time.

My Flight Commander was not above twisting the rules. One day he asked me to fly him to Kidlington since he was going on leave and it would be a good opportunity for me to practice my cross-country navigation. So far so good; the flight was without incident until he got out of the aircraft at his destination. 'OK,' says he, 'now fly straight home and don't enter my name in your log book and don't refuel before takeoff.'

Well, you might think that may be a bit irregular but it's only a trivial matter. Why shouldn't he get a free trip in quick time to where he wanted to spend his leave? The snag lay in his last instruction – not to refuel before takeoff. We had used very nearly half the tank of petrol, leaving very little safety margin. Officially we always had to refuel before every takeoff from an airfield other than when practising 'circuits and bumps'.

I suppose I could assume that what was being done to me was a great compliment to my navigational skills. I confess that it was with some qualms that I got airborne and headed for Norfolk. With a map spread out on my knee and checking various landmarks as I flew, all went well for the first twenty minutes or so. Then the clouds began to thicken at a pretty low level; so down I went to about five hundred feet. From this low altitude the countryside looks very different from what it does at four thousand feet. Very soon I was hopelessly lost. However I soon spotted a railway line going very nearly in the exact direction I was flying. I also thought I spotted it on the map, so with a sigh of relief I set about following it. I reckoned it should take me to an area around Watton, with which I was adequately familiar and from whence I could fly home. I find it very irritating that I can no longer find on the map the tunnel that was my undoing. Anyway what happened next was that the railway disappeared while I knew I was still far from home and with a fuel gauge indicating I had enough for about ten more minutes' flying. Heading vaguely a little north of east I began to search for a field big enough to land on. Rather than fly any further in a straight line I began a square search, flying for one minute due north, then for one minute due east, then for one and a half minutes due south and one and a half minutes due west.

At last, with my fuel gauge reading empty I spotted a big flat field straight ahead of me. So I made a gentle descent, noticing that it was indeed a beautifully appropriate field, skipped over the boundary hedge and to my astonishment found myself crossing the path of a four-engined bomber just getting airborne. I was some fifty feet from a nasty collision but all was well and as I headed for the control tower my engine spluttered and stopped, allowing me to come to a halt more or less where I thought I should but unable to move an inch further. I'd landed at RAF Honington, about fifteen miles south of my destination. I rang my CO at Bodney, who was relieved to know that both I and my aircraft were safe. He then flew over to make sure that I got back to base without further mishap.

I was involved in just one other small accident when my Flight Commander was flying and I was his pupil/passenger. The grass airfield had runways of a kind – still grass – marked out with drem lights. These gave an adequate amount of light for one to land at night but were only visible if one were approaching at a reasonable angle in order to land. They were invisible from above and very nearly invisible in bright daylight, though they did protrude enough to make them a hazard to the delicate tailwheel of a Master. I was glad that it was my instructor and not I at the controls when we ripped off our tailwheel on one of these things.

I ended my course at Bodney on 21 September and to my surprise was assessed as above the average for my flying skills. God alone knows what the assessment would have been if I'd pranged out of fuel or, worse still, collided with that bomber at Honington.

I was posted forthwith to No. 61 (Spitfire) OTU at Rednal, near Oswestry in Shropshire, but not alas to fly Spitfires. I'd been sent to join X Squadron

– that part of the establishment that was there to help train Spitfire pilots in air gunnery. Our aircraft were Lysanders and Martinets. Our role was drogue towing. The drogue was something like a windsock only much bigger since it had to represent approximately an aircraft and be vaguely similar to the sort of target Spitfire pilots might be engaging. The basic job was incredibly boring but we managed to make it quite exciting with some fun and games; and other excitements came our way which we would never have chosen.

The Martinet was virtually a Master converted to tow drogues. It wasn't a patch on the Lysander, which was an aircraft I came to love. Being a high-winged monoplane the Lizzie had a wonderful view downwards while the shape of the wings meant that the all-round visibility was second to none. With any sort of a wind you could land it across the width of a runway and get airborne in much the same distance. On top of that it was almost as fast as the ancient MkI and MkII Spitfires with which the OTU was equipped. The major snag, which I dare say applied throughout Training Command, was that the best ground crews were all at operational stations looking after the machines that were actually fighting the war.

During the five months I was with X Squadron we experienced three nasty incidents, in two of which I was the pilot involved. The other however was probably the most horrific for the pilot and drogue operator airborne at the time. They'd just got airborne when the fabric of the starboard wing began to peel off. The pilot had gone just too far to be able to put down safely flying straight ahead; so he decided to do a circuit of the airfield and hope to get down before he lost any more fabric (and lift). It was not to be: more and more fabric disappeared until that starboard wing was stripped naked. This was a good deal worse than embarrassing. Handling an aircraft with virtually three-quarters of a wing missing is a lot harder than flying a twin-engined aircraft on one engine. On this occasion all ended well and both pilot and drogue operator were up again next day.

Now this sort of thing is tough for the pilot but think how much worse it is for the drogue operator who has to sit there with his life in your hands and able to do absolutely nothing to help. My own nastiest time was likewise soon after take off in a Lizzie; and I guess it was due to a similar lack of efficiency in the ground crew, though it has to be said that they were dealing with pretty ancient machines.

On 29 January 1943 I took off with my drogue operator to do the usual duty, involving a flight up to the Dee estuary and then turning west to fly to and fro towing the target for the Spit pilots to shoot at. On this occasion the mission was not accomplished. I'd been airborne just over five minutes when smoke began to fill my cockpit and my feet started to get extra warm. I turned round smartly and headed back to base. My log book tells me that this whole flight only lasted fifteen minutes but it felt a great deal longer than that. The main problem was the loss of visibility. The smoke was getting denser and my feet were getting hotter and seeing the ground was getting harder. I judged that my best course was to get on the ground as fast as possible. I was glad that I was so familiar now with the terrain below that I could almost have made it blindfold.

Having arrived over the airfield at Rednal, the next problem was to get down. I began my landing approach but well before touchdown found I could no longer see anything below. That was when I made my big mistake. I slid back the cockpit hood. Immediately the smoke vanished – to be replaced by fire. I'd just time to gauge how I should complete my approach and landing before I got the hood shut again. The flames disappeared from the cockpit and the smoke came back. We got down; it was not a smooth landing but I did fetch up reasonably close to the fire tender. The two of us got out pretty smartly. I learned later that we'd burned fifty-four out of the fifty-six pints of oil on board. And I needed a new pair of trousers. After which I had two days off.

The third incident needs a bit of preparatory explanation. After each exercise on the range we had to drop the drogue so that it could be examined and a report sent back as to the number of holes in it, i.e. the number of hits scored by the trainee Spitfire pilot. In a small hut about two hundred yards inland from the coastal range was the man responsible for picking up the drogue, doing the count and telephoning the results to base. The drogue was attached to the Lizzie or Martinet by about a hundred yards of strong wire cable, which was wound round a winch in the rear cockpit of the plane. It was the pilot's job to cry 'drop' when he thought the drogue would conveniently land reasonably near the hut.

The drogue operator then simply had to pull a lever to release the cable and the drogue with it, which would fall more or less in the right place, depending on the wind conditions and the height and timing of the drop.

To put a bit of fun into our lives the X Squadron pilots set up a competition to see who could drop the drogue closest to the door of the hut without actually hitting it. This was ostensibly to give the bloke doing the pick up less work. It was after all quite a big job to get the cable rolled up again and the drogue analysed – all twenty feet of it.

I'm a competitive sort of person and was determined to win this competition. Various attempts had taken place and the nearest drop had been some twenty feet from the hut. I was sure we could improve on that. The trick of course was to fly low enough so that the moment we dropped our drogue it would hit the ground. Being a hundred yards ahead this required nice judgement. When my chance came I thought I'd got it dead right and cried 'drop'. Nothing happened. Or rather everything happened very fast and not according to plan. My operator had pulled the lever promptly but there was no release. Normally if that happened one would simply go up higher, do a circuit and try again. If absolutely necessary it would be possible to cut the cable; for what was quite impractical was to land with the cable and drogue still attached.

The result of the failed drop was first that I felt a juddering strain on the aircraft. I gave her full throttle and I still felt that I was in danger of stalling. I seemed to be towing not a drogue but a tank. It was most uncomfortable. Having given the engine all the power available I spared a moment to look down and backwards. What I saw was my drogue entangled in a barbed wire fence with which we were having a tug of war. Fascinated, and keeping my Lizzie some fifty feet above the ground, I saw the fence poles gradually give up the struggle and leave the earth one by one to follow me and my drogue into the air with many yards of barbed wire coming along for the ride.

Luckily there seemed to be no human inhabitant of the fields; no furious farmer to get me into trouble or to risk serious injury himself. I was for the moment winning the tug of war but was well aware that the situation might alter for the worse at any moment. The drag of my cable grew greater. The risk of stalling loomed closer. A stall at

this height would mean a violent plunge down the fifty feet to the ground. I suppose that had I seriously thought we were about to crash I could have put the nose hard down and made a reasonably soft landing, though the terrain was far from ideal. At least this time my drogue operator had something to do as he furiously struggled to make the releasing gear work. The climax came when the cable snapped. A small portion of it whipped back and gave us a slap; most of it stayed on the ground all tangled up with the barbed wire that had recently divided two fields.

I flew back in rather sober mood and didn't try again to beat the dropping record.

The only other break from our monotonous job came when I was invited to fly one of our WAAFs to Exeter in a Master. This time there were no navigational problems or indeed any other, for we had a fine day for the trip and we could converse amicably throughout the flight. My WAAF was not used to flying. I invited her to say whether she'd like to have some aerobatic fun while on the journey. 'Yes,' she said, 'I'd like that – as long as you don't do a loop.'

Now a well-executed loop gives pleasure to the pilot and would hardly be noticed by a passenger who wasn't looking outside the plane. My passenger thought it would make her feel sick. So I went through a complete repertoire of slow rolls, chandelles, steep turns and even a spin, dropping a thousand feet in quick time before pulling out, then finally one flick roll – this last a manoeuvre that was prohibited in many aircraft since it puts considerable strain on the wings. After each of my efforts my WAAF said, 'More, please. Try something else.' So I said, 'Close your eyes then; and promise me not to open them until I tell you. Then you can guess what we've done.'

To this she agreed and I put the nose down and got our airspeed up to around three hundred miles per hour, pulled back on the stick and executed as perfect a loop as I'd ever done. Having eased down to our normal cruising speed and flying now straight and level, I told her to open her eyes and tell me what sort of manoeuvre she thought we'd done.

'Well,' she replied, 'you went down a bit fast and then you slowed it and as far as I can see that's all you did.'

'That', I told her, 'was your dreaded loop.'

'OK,' she said, 'then will you do it again?' Which I did, only this time it was not quite so well executed. From her point of view it was probably all the more enjoyable for that.

CHAPTER XI

Rednal was quite unlike any other station I'd been on. In later life I got to know Shropshire fairly well but this was my first time in that county. I made great friends with a kindly woman who lived just outside the station and who offered to do my laundry for me: an offer I promptly accepted. She did this for a paltry sum and I was very glad neither to have to take it home nor to do it myself.

I was usually free on a Sunday evening and soon decided that I'd cycle into Oswestry, about five miles away, to Evensong. This was partly because I'd met and immediately taken to the vicar, Prebendary E. More Darling. I rode a sporty kind of bike and tried each week to beat my previous speed record for the trip. On one glorious occasion I was able to get behind a coach that was going all the way to Oswestry and beyond. I managed thirty miles an hour for the trip and never quite topped that record.

The surrounding countryside was very beautiful. Many years later Sylvia and I thought quite seriously of buying our retirement house in the county. From a pilot's point of view the one menace was the hill known as the Wrekin. It stood way up above the fairly flat surrounding countryside and in dirty weather it had claimed the lives of several pilots. We treated it with enormous respect and during my time at Rednal no one flew into it.

Early in 1943 I had one of my nastiest experiences among my fellow countrymen during the time I was in uniform. A friend and I decided to have a night out in Liverpool. I think I consented slightly against my better judgement; in other words I hadn't the guts to say that a night on the town held no attractions for me. The theory was that we'd go find a jolly pub, have a few beers and with luck pick up a couple of girls.

We had no trouble getting to Liverpool or in finding what at first sight looked like a jolly pub. Entering in our usual carefree (and possibly somewhat swaggering) style we approached the bar. The place was packed out: there were one or two Tommies and a great many civilians. Wherever I'd been before the pilot's wings on my breast had guaranteed a warm and even enthusiastic reception. Not so on this occasion. Someone in the crowd said something like 'Get the bastards!' and the whole crowd turned towards us and advanced in a highly menacing manner. We decided without a moment's consultation that discretion was the better part of valour. In short we turned and ran, pursued for a short way by some of our more persistent adversaries. Not having yet had even our first drink and being young and fit, we had no difficulty in getting away. But my heart was pounding and I was in a state of abject terror compared with which my contretemps with the fire in my Lizzie was as nothing.

Had we been older and wiser, or just better informed, we might have realised that the Liverpudleans had had quite a pasting for several nights in a row from the bombers of the Luftwaffe. The locals considered that the RAF had made a pretty poor effort at defending them. In that particular environment at that precise time the pilots of the RAF were regarded as abominable. Sometimes, we learned, it's better not to be in uniform.

At last it happened. I'd finished my time with X Squadron and was transferred to the main part of the OTU and began my training on Spitfires. There were only a couple of days to wait, during which I had to take a written exam on the Spitfire, learn and be checked out on my cockpit drill, satisfy my new CO on a Master that I was a competent pilot in practice not just theory and finally master the radio and other systems peculiar to this wonderful aeroplane. It was on 2 February 1943 that I did my 'first solo on type' as it had to be entered in my log book. This was the moment I'd looked forward to for so many years. The experience was every bit as marvellous as I'd hoped. I suppose there's always a slight anxiety as one takes off for the first time in any new type of aircraft. But the Spitfire is such a beautiful machine that in next to no time it felt almost like an extension of my body, responding smoothly and instantly to whatever I desired. The first landing – especially in a Spitfire – is also a wee bit hairy: mine was not perfect but not far short. I never found landing a Spit as hard as landing a Harvard in spite of the fact that there was that awkward lack of forward vision at touchdown. (The Spitfire's nose totally hid the view straight ahead when in the stalling position.)

I'm sure I'd been told that I shouldn't stay up for more than one hour and forty-five minutes but on my second flight my joy simply made me oblivious of time. I'd actually been airborne for two hours and ten minutes when I finally touched down. As my aircraft settled on the tarmac the engine spluttered and stopped. I was completely out of fuel. Only once more in my whole flying career was I airborne for so long in a Spitfire: that was to be eighteen months later when fitted with a ninety-gallon auxiliary drop tank.

Over the next two months we practised every kind of flight we'd be likely to use on an operational squadron. On looking back I find that on roughly every eighth flight there was something wrong with the aircraft. Of course they were all old ex-Battle of Britain machines and even in this main part of the OTU we didn't have the RAF's best mechanics. Nor of course did we have its best pilots. Apart from my lucky escape from running out of fuel while airborne I did one other awful thing, landing at the very end of my time on the course at an away station with my undercarriage retracted. This of course was a legitimate manoeuvre when forced to land in rough country but it never did the Spitfire much good. I consider myself extremely lucky not to have been failed. I suppose I must have had some compensating virtues, for my chief flying instructor assessed me as above average.

It was while at Rednal that I witnessed a fatal accident for the first time. We were doing some practice formation flying and putting in some cine-gun attacks on each other's flights. The cine-gun was operated by pressing a special button on the stick, thus recording what one might have hit if one had been firing the guns. The camera was also operated automatically whenever the guns were fired. I'd just landed and taxied in to my dispersal place when I looked up and was horrified to see one Spitfire drop down straight on top of another, slicing off its whole tailplane, causing it to plummet to the ground, where it smashed into pieces. The pilot was killed instantly. His poor colleague managed to get down safely. Perhaps he'd rather not have done. In any case he couldn't face flying again.

This tragedy was followed a few days later by the one and only military funeral that I shared in. Once we were on ops, death was of course more to be expected and funerals were quiet affairs – mostly on the other side of the Channel. But for this occasion we gave it the works: the body was in a flag-draped coffin, drawn by horses on some sort of gun-carriage. I was among those slow-marching behind along a seemingly endless route from the airfield to the parish church. I remember nothing of the service itself but I remember weeping very slightly but with intense feeling as we proceeded accompanied by the station band playing the Dead March of Saul.

I had mixed feelings about leaving Rednal, where on the whole I'd been very happy. I was certainly looking forward eagerly to joining an operational Spitfire squadron but I was aware that the dangerous part of my RAF life was now about to begin.

CHAPTER XII

After a week's leave I moved to Hawkinge in Kent, where I joined 41 Fighter Squadron, which had just been re-equipped with the very latest MkXII Spitfires. For the first time our aircraft were powered by the Rolls Royce Griffon engine, which developed 1750 horsepower in comparison with the 1280 horsepower of the Merlin 45 which powered the MkVb.

This enormous increase in power was immensely valuable. The MkXII had clipped wings as had the later MkVs. The nose was longer and there were two long bumps in the engine cowling needed to accommodate the bigger engine. However to an untrained eye and even to most German pilots it would be hard to distinguish the two types in flight. Since we could turn just as well, climb five hundred odd feet a minute faster and fly straight and level some fifty miles per hour faster than the MkV at our best height, we expected to cause some havoc when engaged with enemy fighters. The Griffon engine revolved in the opposite direction to the Merlin; this meant that the torque felt on takeoff would inevitably cause the plane to crash if the rudder was trimmed as if for a Merlin. Trimming was effected by adjusting a small wheel tucked in low down to the pilot's left.

It was regarded as most important that none of our aircraft should risk being brought down over enemy territory before we were thoroughly trained to take advantage of our superiority. The snag about this cautious behaviour was that we were restricted to purely defensive patrols over the Channel, weather and shipping reconnaissances and the occasional escort job without ever crossing the French coast.

Soon after we'd got our MkXIIs, 91 Squadron was also equipped with them and later we would form with them a Spit XII wing at Tangmere.

We were only at Hawkinge for seventeen days. Then we were posted to Biggin Hill, Kent, where Fighter Command had its HQ. Our CO was determined to demonstrate in this illustrious place what a superb lot of pilots we were. He therefore ordered that we should land – the whole squadron – in tight formation. We'd practised tight formation flying and I enjoyed that very much but this was something different, which we'd never done before. In the air you can achieve what looks from below like incredibly close flying because you keep a few feet below the aircraft ahead of you while tucked in so that your leading edge is only about two feet behind the trailing edge of the wing in front of you. Once you hit the deck you are of course liable to collide with the bloke in front if either of you makes the slightest error.

On touching down on the runway at Biggin Hill the bloke in front of me touched his brakes. I hit him immediately. Luckily no one was hurt but both aircraft were extensively damaged. Since neither of us pilots got a rocket, I suspect that it was our intrepid CO who was hauled over the coals. In any case we never tried that exploit again.

I cannot for the life of me think why we were sent to Biggin Hill, unless perhaps it was so that some bigwigs could assess our competence. Anyway we only stayed there for a week, during which we did no operational flying. Indeed the only time I went up was to take part in some formation flying practice. Then on 28 May we were transferred to Friston, a wartime fighter station without runways or any permanent RAF accommodation. I loved this place, which was perched on the edge of the cliffs just to the west of Beachy Head in Sussex. On this first occasion we were only there for three weeks but were destined to return twice more, always with the defence of Eastbourne as our primary task. For some strange reason a few German fighter-bombers would dash across the channel and drop a bomb or two on the town now and then probably because it was a large and easily spotted target within easy range of the airfields in Northern France. It had no military significance; I suspect it was merely to keep up the morale of the Luftwaffe that these raids happened at all. The press – or maybe it was the Ministry of Information – dubbed these incursions 'sneak raids'. Our Spit XIIs might have been designed to deal with them and ultimately we did see them off.

The MkXII had in addition to the powerful Griffon engine a Coffman starter. Before this invention came in the engine could only be started with the help of an external battery, a large, cumbersome affair which had to be wheeled up and plugged in by ground staff and then of course unplugged and taken away before the aircraft could move off. The Coffman starter was like a gun that forced the engine to turn at high speed by firing a cartridge. The magazine held six cartridges but in skilful hands only one was ever needed. The trick was to get the mixture exactly right at the moment of firing. If the mixture was too weak one could enrich it and fire a second cartridge. If it was already too rich you might have to fire two or three more cartridges to get rid of the extra fuel before the engine would fire. The mixture (of air and fuel) was controlled by a plunger. One downward thrust followed by about half of a second thrust was about right. So the trick was to give it one full thrust and then fire the starter while pushing the plunger hard down for the second thrust. That way a moment was bound to come when the engine was turning over with the correct mixture, when it would immediately spring into life.

The cooling system depended on swift movement through the air, so that it was a dangerous practice to have one's engine running for more than a minute or two while stationary. The most efficient way by far of getting airborne in the minimum of time was therefore to be lined up ready for takeoff with brakes off and alert for the signal which would be followed by the starting method just described. I believe I once captured the record for the quickest take off ever to intercept a sneak raider. I had for some time kept my eyes glued to the watchtower, where the man on duty would order us to scramble by firing a Very pistol high but in our direction. On this particular occasion I saw him answer the 'phone and reach for the pistol. At once I did my one and a half thrusts and fired my Coffman starter and was rolling forward by the time the Very light burst above us. My Number One was a mite behind me. We headed south at full throttle but on this occasion had no luck. The raiders had turned tail and had too great a lead for us to catch them.

Indeed we enjoyed little success in the form of enemy aircraft destroyed. What we did do was to mount patrols of two aircraft which kept continuous watch over the sea for some thirty miles east to thirty miles west of Beachy Head; which was enough to stop the sneak raiders from approaching.

On 21 June we moved to Westhampnett, a satellite aerodrome of Tangmere, which was one of the busiest of our fighter stations and which also housed the top-secret Lysander squadron, whose intrepid pilots flew by night to land agents in France and bring them back after their jobs were completed The move signalled the end of that cautious period when we were forbidden to risk getting shot down over enemy territory. It was now time for us to go on the offensive.

CHAPTER XIII

By now I'd got 450 flying hours behind me, with the last fifty being on Spit XIIs. I felt thoroughly at home in the air and was aware that I was almost reliving my dream experience (often had from childhood) that I could just flap my hands and then fly like a bird. The exhilaration was intense. I surmise that every one of us felt the same. We were an odd bunch. My Flight Commander was Doug Hone. He was a warm-hearted and excellent leader but he didn't stay with us long. I think he was probably given his own squadron but all I know for sure is that he left 41 in June and was replaced in July by one Pinky Glen, who was probably the most inspiring of the various officers under whom I served and who later was to come back as CO of the squadron.

Other notable characters were Tom Slack, then a flying officer, later to be my Flight Commander. He was a cartoonist of great talent. One of my secret sorrows was that I was never the subject of any of his witty drawings. I can still vividly recall his impressions of Peter Cowell and of Gizzie, of whom more anon, of Jackie Fisher, a sergeant pilot a few months senior to me in the squadron and several others. Jackie was newly married and usually managed to get his wife settled in some nearby accommodation, so that however busy we were he was able to enjoy some connubial bliss. Indeed from time to time the bliss was a bit overdone: time in bed for him was more exhausting than time with the squadron.

Two other NCO pilots, with whom I resumed contact many years after the war was over, were Jim Payne and Peter Wall, two good friends, with whom and with whose wives Sylvia and I have had some happy times together. Joe Birbeck was about my age – possibly a bit younger – but had lied his way into the RAF at the age of sixteen. He was at this time a flying officer and more often than not my Number One.

We never flew operationally except in pairs or in greater numbers. This was to ensure that we could defend each other and keep a sharp lookout in all directions. When we flew as a squadron the CO would lead a central formation of four aircraft and each of the Flight Commanders would lead their own four on the flanks. For most of the time we kept that formation right through an offensive operation but it was up to any Number One to peel off and attack an enemy aircraft, telling the CO and the rest of us what he was doing. He would automatically be followed by his Number Two.

The principal offensive operation was the sweep, which involved the whole squadron flying as a unit, more often than not as an escort to or distraction from a bomber force attacking targets in Northern France or shipping around the ports. Sometimes we simply went looking for trouble, hoping to spot enemy aircraft. I found it quite exciting just to spot the odd Messerschmidt 109 or Focker-Wulf 190, even when it was not practicable to have a go at them.

By far the most exciting kind of operation, I felt, was the rhubarb. Now and again the odd pilot who had achieved Number One status would get permission to go with his Number Two on a low level recco over Northern France just seeking out likely targets on the ground and hoping also to encounter the odd German fighter which could be brought down, we hoped.

It was on one of these excursions that I got into my first and arguably my worst bit of trouble. Joe Birbeck and I had ranged around for about twenty minutes over France and had hit nothing more important than a defenceless water tower. It was time to go home; so we headed north leaving France close to St Valery, hedge-hopping, as we had been for most of the time. The theory of course was that no anti-aircraft gunner would be able to react swiftly enough to hit us.

On this occasion it didn't turn out that way: as we crossed the coast there was an almighty bang and everything changed. After the roar and racket of the past quarter of an hour there was suddenly total silence. There was glass everywhere except in the instrument panel where it belonged. My right arm wouldn't obey my commands but hung loose at my side. Almost every dial, indicator and gauge in front of me had gone haywire. Not a squeak from the radio; not a murmur from the engine; no wind noise; total silence; and around me total chaos. I was stone deaf.

I didn't consciously count my blessings at that moment but they were many and marvellous. For a start I was still in the air, not the sea; the engine was obviously still running and all the controls were working. It was simple enough to fly one-handed, for both my feet were OK. I was to discover later that had the shell that hit me entered one inch higher or lower it would have severed some of the vital cables leading to the rudder and elevators. Most vital of all to my mind after the explosion was that there was Joe just ahead and to my right, obviously OK and able to lead me home. The one instrument that was working properly was the air speed indicator.

I'd received a direct hit by a forty-millimetre anti-aircraft shell that exploded on the armour plate behind my head. Two or three inches further forward and it would have blown my head off. Now I was flying fairly comfortably just keeping formation with my Number One until we got back to Westhampnett. I've never checked it out but have the impression that he was quite unaware of the extent of my trouble. He landed first and I circled the airfield and could see no sign of crash wagon or ambulance below. I was a bit bothered by this as I didn't know how I'd get the undercarriage down or whether I'd know if it was down and locked. I didn't fancy doing a wheels-up landing but probably I should have at least seriously considered it or alternatively flown across to Tangmere to make my touchdown on a really big station with all the facilities.

In the end I flew over my airfield a couple of times, waggling my wings. I then climbed to about three thousand feet in order to execute the quite difficult manoeuvre of lowering the undercarriage with my left hand. That wasn't easy because the control lever was situated at floor level on the right hand side of the seat. To do this I had to leave the aircraft to fly itself while I contorted myself and finally managed to grab and operate the control.

Now how, I wondered, was I to get down in the space available without the use of brakes? I experimented in the air to see if I could work the brake lever with my left hand; I could not. In the Spitfire the control in question was a lever tucked into the right-hand-side of the hoop that topped the joystick. The trick then obviously was to come in over the boundary hedge so low that I could touch down almost at once and then cut the engine. It was now that I greatly appreciated the fact that I'd still got a functioning air speed indicator; thus I could cross the hedge just above stalling speed and touch down as planned. In fact the landing seemed so good that I didn't cut the engine. My Spit behaved superbly, stopping just short of the further hedge. I turned and started taxiing towards our dispersal area.

Suddenly I realised with enormous relief that I was hearing perfectly well. I suppose sound had been returning gradually over the last ten minutes or so. Then I glanced down at my limp right arm and received a shock. Blood was welling out over the top of my flying gauntlet. At the same moment someone was getting the canopy hood off and I yelled 'Get the blood wagon' and promptly fainted.

The next thing I knew I was in the back of an ambulance with our MO, Doc. Burnett sitting beside me, just having completed the application of a tourniquet to my damaged arm. For the first time I became aware that I wasn't comfortable. I soon found myself tucked up in bed in St Richard's hospital, Chichester. My only vivid memory of my hospital stay was the procedure surrounding the surgery on my arm. In the theatre or an adjoining room I had a mask over my face, a horrible smell up my nose and my left arm raised for as long as I could hold it up. I also had to count aloud for as long as I was conscious. I was out for a long time. When the surgeon visited me to tell me all had gone very well, he handed me a lump of metal, which I've carefully preserved as a souvenir, and told me this was by far the biggest bit he'd got out of me; it had been quite a long job to find and remove smaller slivers. I had seventeen days in hospital altogether and then a fortnight's sick leave.

On this event my flying log book simply recorded: 'RHUBARB. WOUNDED SLIGHTLY BY FLAK. A/C CAT. B'. I was proud of my little war wound and believed at the time that I'd got off extremely lightly, which in a sense I had. I was not to know that the results of that explosion would make such a vast difference to the second half of my life.

CHAPTER XIV

Before my sick leave came to an end I decided to do a bit of dinghy sailing on the Thames. I took my brave sister Mary with me. We walked to Wheatley, took a train to Oxford and hired the dinghy near Folly Bridge. There was a stiff breeze but because of the many trees along the river banks it was fluky. Mary had never sailed before and I'd never before sailed in conditions like these. All went well for a time but a sudden violent gust capsized us. We were in no danger and the boat was quickly righted but neither of us was keen to prolong the sail. We returned, looking and feeling a sorry sight, delivered up the dinghy with due apologies for the wetness of the sail and trudged to the station.

Here at least, I thought, we could get ourselves a hot drink while waiting for the train. There was indeed a canteen on the platform, staffed by one of the voluntary services, which did so much to ease our lives in those days. The only trouble was that there were a great many soldiers crowding round. There was plenty of time to wait before the next train for Wheatley was due but we were shivering with cold in our sodden clothes, so I had no compunction in pressing as speedily as I could to a vantage point where I could catch the eye of one of the women serving us to ask for two cups of tea.

I was astonished to find that my attempts to attract attention were studiously, deliberately and pointedly ignored. This was, I think, the first time I'd gone to one of these canteens out of uniform. I'd grown accustomed to receiving instant and smiling service. Those wings on my breast worked magic. Now when I was in greater need of a comforting cuppa than ever before and when I was accompanied by a damsel in distress, no one took a blind bit of notice of us. At last I called out, 'Hey! Do you mind serving us? I've been waiting much longer than some of these chaps.'

'These chaps', was the reply, 'are in the King's uniform. When you're in it I'll be glad to serve you.' No doubt I should have come back with some remark about the courage of conscientious objectors. Of course I didn't, but I gave her a piece of my mind and of the truth. Whereupon she had the grace to blush, apologise and serve us quickly.

I was back in the air on 25 August, getting used to flying again and doing a bit of practice on ground targets with my cine-gun. Two days later I was flying with the whole squadron on a sweep escorting Forts (the American B17 or Flying Fortress). We had quite a dodgy time and from our point of view a sad one. The Forts carried out their mission successfully but we lost two pilots, one of whom baled out; the other was missing – I've no idea if he survived. We'd spent a lot of time at full throttle and were therefore low in fuel by the time the action was over. We flew to Ford, which was our nearest RAF station and incidentally the one with the longest runway in the south.

When a football team gets badly defeated the first idea to hit the club seems to be to sack the manager. Whether that was the reason why we lost our CO I've no idea. Anyway before the month was out we had a new one, S/L B. Ingham. Did he go on to win his K. and undying fame as Margaret Thatcher's press secretary? I don't really think it was the same Ingham but he had some of the same qualities. I do know that he was a first-rate CO and led us to some famous victories.

We celebrated the fourth anniversary of the outbreak of war with a sweep giving close escort cover to thirty-six Marauders (light bombers) and for safety landed at Tangmere on our return. Next day we did a similar mission. This time Joe Birbeck and I were lucky enough to be able to engage a pair of FW190s that were attacking some Spit Vs below us. He shot one down and almost at the same moment I was hit, I thought, by flak. My engine temperature gauge began to climb; so I headed straight for home – or rather for Ford, where I landed without trouble, though the temperature of the engine was now dangerously high. As I'd suspected there was a hole in the radiator, which I put down to flak but learned later that in fact the damage was caused by bullet clips – presumably emanating from the successful guns of my Number One.

On 9 September we were engaged in providing air cover to an assault force off Boulogne. This, I presume, was to persuade Hitler that the ultimate invasion would be launched in the Pas de Calais rather than in Normandy. Maybe also we were trying to help the Russians a bit by persuading the Germans that they must keep a large force in the West. We were over France nearly every day this month. On one occasion, flying as a wing with 91 Squadron our Spit XIIs destroyed five enemy aircraft and damaged another for the loss of one aircraft from 91 Squadron.

On another occasion I was woken in bed in the early morning to be told

I'd got six minutes to get airborne in a whole squadron scramble. In fact we managed the feat in ten minutes and I don't believe it could have been done any faster. The panic was that we were required to go and refuel at West Malling and then escort a bomber force that was just getting airborne to attack targets in Merville. When we got to the target area it was covered in ten-tenths cloud, so we returned to base.

The 26 September was celebrated as Battle of Britain Day. 41 Squadron played its part by buzzing the city of Chichester in close formation and generally displaying our aerobatic skills at low altitude. Nowadays, in the twenty-first century, the noise of powerful low-flying fighter planes is very disturbing if not positively frightening. But I doubt if many people felt like that about the modest roar of twelve Spitfires demonstrating their pride and joy in their machines at that date. Intriguingly many years later I saw a photograph of part of this incident in the Bader Arms at Tangmere. True, it only shows one flight of six aircraft; but they are clearly ours as the squadron letters 'EB' on the fuselage demonstrate. And this was the only occasion when we did this demonstration over Chichester.

Next day we had a most exciting time: escorting seventy-two Marauders, we were engaged no less than six times by German fighters. At one point Joe and I broke off to follow two Messerschmidts which dived straight through our formation. They were, it turned out, a decoy to draw us into a trap; the trap consisted of some thirty ME109s and FW190s all of which were soon after us. This was the one and only traditional dogfight in which I was ever engaged. It was fast and furious and had the German pilots been of top quality they'd probably have shot us both down. As it was we managed to avoid even getting hit and for our part we damaged three of theirs. In my own case I got a good burst in on a FW190 and saw his cockpit hood blow away. I reckon that was a probable victory, for if the pilot had jettisoned his hood it would presumably mean he intended to bale out. Back at home the *Oxford Mail* put in a column about our scrap, which I suppose was based on an interview I had with a reporter at the time.

CHAPTER XV

Soon after this exciting day I discovered I'd been promoted to F/Sgt – a pretty meaningless business in terms of responsibilities but it was worth a couple of bob a week in the pay packet. It did however prove valuable in quite another way. My mother, with ulterior motives, I'm sure, wrote to Sylvia's parents about this and that and mentioned my promotion. This in turn led to my first letter from Sylvia, who wrote to congratulate me, thus beginning a correspondence that lasted for ever.

On 4 October the squadron shifted to the mother station at Tangmere. Some time that winter, while on leave at home, I bought an old car – an Austin 6. It had been used for some time as a taxi and was rather decrepit. It cost me around £40. It was worth a lot more than that to me, but because petrol was severely rationed the demand for such a vehicle was slight. With a little helpful advice from a fellow pilot, I taught myself to drive by practising on the perimeter track around the aerodrome.

On 15 October Winston Churchill was for some reason visiting Ford – that station with the mile-long runway, which was a life-saver for me on several occasions. Just in case word of this visit had reached the Germans, our squadron was given the task of providing air cover for him. This meant that we spent an hour and a quarter patrolling just south of the airfield while the PM was inspecting whatever it was he was interested in on the ground.

Five days later, flying as a wing with 91 Squadron we had our most successful day ever. Maddeningly I played very little part in it. We did two separate sweeps over Bernay, Le Havre, Poix and Beauvais. We encountered a very large formation of German fighters, over 120 of them. Our wing score was nine destroyed and two damaged for no loss on our part, though my own Number One was hit and I had to escort him home before the best bit of the fight took place. Intriguingly our Wing Commander Richard Harries had flying as his Number Two no less a person than Group Captain Chisholm, Station Commander of RAF Tangmere. This was the only occasion when I was aware of such a high-ranking officer going on an offensive operation. He certainly chose a good day. It was in fact the last time the Germans put up a large force of fighters against us. They still had plenty of aircraft and pilots but were desperately short of fuel. Whenever we were in squadron strength they kept well out of our way though we occasionally spotted a few FW190s a great way off.

For the most part we were escorting medium bombers, Bostons, Mitchells or Marauders. Usually they flew in groups of seventy-two. These were aircraft of the US Army Air Corps, which had the major responsibility for the daylight bombing of targets in France, which tended to be railway marshalling yards, fuel depots and the northern ports. Sometimes the flak was intense but opposition from the air was usually negligible. I recall that the heaviest flak I experienced came from the Channel Isles. If I had the chance – as for instance when on a rhubarb – I'd sometimes glance down and see the shells coming up at me in time to dodge them.

At the end of an eventful month I had a fortnight's leave, which I spent at home; home now being the Old Vicarage at Cuddesdon, a lovely old house which was really was vast.

The only thing I remember about this leave was that Sylvia came to stay with us. I think I behaved very badly, found very little time to be alone with her and very little to talk about. My mother in particular and my family in general were all expecting the romance I'd not yet started. This made me withdraw in a way I hope I wouldn't have done if I'd had her to myself. My courtship, now I look back at it, would have been incomprehensible to the young people of today. I never spoke a word of love – still less a word of any sexual significance until I'd got her father's consent to ask her hand in marriage. That stage was still some way off.

CHAPTER XVI

Winter was now upon us and Spitfires don't have any heating system. (Nor for that matter did our four-engined bombers, whose crews had to sit for hours in cramped quarters and intense cold just to add to the discomfort of being shot at by anti-aircraft guns for half the time they were over Germany at night.) It was vital for us to keep our hands warm; in cold weather this meant wearing three pairs of gloves – silk next to the skin, wool over the silk and finally big leather gauntlets.

Most of us were happiest when we operated in small formations; best of all was the rhubarb. I flew several of these as Number Two to Joe Birbeck. In December I got my commission as Pilot Officer and also became for the first time a Number One, thus able to be in charge when on a rhubarb with a Number Two to take care of me.

Getting my commission meant moving out of the sergeants' mess into the officers'. It also meant wearing a more comfortable uniform and having marginally *less* money to spend. The P/O's pay was a wee bit more than the F/Sgt's but there were mess bills and one had to pay for one's own uniform. As a matter of fact I was soon appreciably better off because I fell into partnership at bridge with our famous intelligence officer. He was F/Lt the Earl of Guisborough, known to everyone as 'Gizzie'. In many ways a remarkable man, he was not a notably successful IO. Indeed I believe every wartime CO of 41 Squadron had tried to get rid of him. But he was a friend of Lord Trenchard, the Father of the RAF; and with that influence behind him he was immovable. He had found the place where he was comfortable and had no intention of quitting it. That was a joy to most of us, since he was a truly loveable character, full of good humour and a very competent bridge player. When I arrived on the scene he'd just lost his regular bridge partner and was looking round for a replacement. As luck would have it I filled the bill nicely and we set up a partnership that was to last for almost a year. Since we played almost every evening and since we nearly always won, even at the modest rate of a penny a hundred we used to earn something like an extra five shillings a week each.

Gizzie used to go everywhere on a clapped-out bicycle and in the most ancient and tatty of uniforms. What little hair he had was never tidy but he carried good cheer wherever he went. I once asked him, 'Aren't you really quite a wealthy man?'

He said, 'I don't think so but it depends how you count wealth. I can't afford to run a car. I have to think twice before taking a train to go up to town and sit in the Lords. And I'm not sure how I'd manage if I didn't have a good bridge partner to ensure I can pay my mess bills.'

'Don't you own any land?' I asked.

'Yes indeed I do', he replied. 'I own the town of Guisborough – all except the water works.'

'Surely then', I went on, 'that must bring you in more than a few pennies?'

'I'm not sure what the exact figures are at the moment', Gizzie confided. 'Let's say the income is around £1 million.'

'Isn't that enough to be going on with?' I asked.

'Well, it would be of course,' he said, 'were it not for the outgoings. I have to keep everything up. I reckon that costs me just *over* a million.'

'Couldn't you sell the odd bit now and then?', I said in all innocence, only to receive the stern reply: 'You never part with capital – least of all with land – if you're a Guisborough. If I were to start down that road there would be no end to it and I would have my father turning in his grave.'

I never raised the subject again but was glad to help keep solvent a man who was so evidently poorer than myself.

Looking through the entries in my flying log book for December I notice that I did an exceptionally large number of test flights. Some of these were just ten-minute affairs, when either everything was OK or the aircraft was in some way seriously out of order, when a hasty landing would be essential. These test flights were virtually the only ones we did in isolation. By this time it was so unlikely that we'd be bounced by a Hun, that we really didn't need the protection provided by operating in pairs. When on my own with no authority to prevent me I found it possible to engage in some very enjoyable flying. On one occasion I flew to Cuddesdon and buzzed the village from one direction after another. It only took just over ten minutes to get there and a flight of forty-five minutes was regarded as quite normal for a thorough test flight.

On another occasion when the weather was perfect I climbed to twenty-six thousand feet and found I could see virtually the whole of the British Isles, the Channel and most of Northern France spread out below me. I'd never before had an experience remotely like this. I remember thinking what a wonderful world we inhabited. As I write this fifty-seven years later that sort of view has become a commonplace. That wonderful sight however still remains in my memory with its attached emotion; I imagine it will now stay with me till I die.

On 14 January we were over France in the morning and again in the afternoon, escorting medium bombers. The target in the afternoon was Cherbourg harbour, which was defended by extremely accurate and intense flak. It seemed quite miraculous that no one was hit, for explosions were going on all around us all the time we were in the target area.

Next month the whole squadron was temporarily withdrawn from ops to polish up our skills as fighter pilots. We were posted to Southend in Essex and spent our time doing mock dogfights with cine-gun and air-to-air firing on drogues. One of my mock dogfights was with Charlie van Goens, a Dutchman who later became my regular Number Two. Another was with F/Lt Burne, who had joined us recently from Training Command. He had an artificial leg, having lost his own in a pre-war flying accident. He had a wonderful handlebar moustache and a great sense of humour. I remember once when we were in a Chichester pub he asked the barmaid if she'd mind his putting a leg up on the bar as it was troubling him. She gave him her OK but got rather more than she bargained for when he pulled up a trouser leg, unstrapped the tin limb and placed it on the bar.

It was at about this time that my father broke the exciting news that he was to be made a bishop. This seemed to be the destiny of most principals of Cuddesdon. It still came as quite a surprise to me because I was well aware of the enormous amount of admin bishops seemed to have to deal with. My father was not, in my view, a good administrator. He couldn't cope with a secretary and wrote all his letters by hand. He was also somewhat too rigid in his views on sexual matters to be able, I thought, to give the lead necessary in a time when divorce was becoming more acceptable. He had to my knowledge forbidden one of his students to attend the wedding of his sister because she was marrying a divorced man whose former wife was still living. However the bishopric he had accepted was that of Brechin in Scotland, where the admin was very slight and the clergy whom he had to shepherd were less than thirty in number.

It was about this time that I first flew operationally as a Number One. This was not the best of occasions to mark my new status. First we had to climb through ten-tenths cloud for four thousand feet. Then when we'd reached the target area the mission was aborted for the obvious reason that the bomber boys couldn't hope to hit their targets through all that cloud. So we had to get back down through it again.

To climb (or descend) through thick cloud the squadron could perform in either of two ways. We could close up and fly in close formation: this required great concentration but at least if you kept really close to the aircraft on which you were formating you were bound to get through in the end. Alternatively we would be set a course, an air speed and a rate of climb and fly in our usual widely spaced operational formation. This was fine for short ascents. It meant total concentration on one's instruments. Unless you do a lot of instrument flying there is a horrible tendency, at the first sight of the sun shining through the thinning cloud above, to take your eyes off your instruments, feeling 'At last I'm out of this.' That is the moment when you can find yourself in a spin, as I did once when on a weather recco over the French coast.

Spinning of course was something all pilots learned to deal with early in their flying training and at OTU I had learned to spin and get out of a spin in a Spitfire. What I had never done was to practice spinning in a Spit XII down through ten thousand feet of ten-tenths cloud. When I finally had to do this for real because I'd made the stupid mistake referred to, it was as alarming as any other experience of my life. I broke out of cloud at around five hundred feet and doing some four hundred miles per hour. I managed to get into straight and level flight just above the waves and within sight of the Channel Isles, where I was well aware that there were plenty of anti-aircraft guns.

CHAPTER XVII

Early in March 1944 the Squadron moved for the second time to Friston, where we stayed for six weeks.

It was at this time that the Allied air assault on German targets in France was stepped up; on one occasion over one thousand American bombers were involved in a single raid. Our own squadron now began penetrating up to one hundred miles inland escorting medium bombers or just engaged in fighter sweeps. We sighted very few enemy aircraft, though there was often quite a lot of flak about. In the middle of the month I had a brief spell in hospital with finger trouble; not the usual kind meaning, in RAF slang, carelessness, but the removal of a whitlow from under a fingernail. On the face of it, this was a very simple operation done under gas, but I remember it as one of the nastiest experiences of my life. This was because while officially unconscious I dreamed I was suffering the tortures of the damned in a hell that would never end. I still recall the feeling of absolute certainty that I was doomed to be in severe pain for ever and ever.

I had a few days' leave after coming out of hospital and visited Sylvia and her parents in York, where they now lived. We went to see a production of the Mikado. About the opera I recall nothing at all. On the way home Sylvia and I walked arm in arm for the very first time. It's hard to imagine how restrained we – and no doubt many others – were in sexual relationships in those far off days. I've no doubt that by this time both Sylvia's parents and mine must have been quite clear about our future marriage. We ourselves had said nothing about love, let alone marriage or indeed any other kind of relationship though we were obviously becoming close friends. Looking back to this time it seems strange to me that whereas I spoke quite openly to Betty Jones about our relationship, I had up to this time said nothing at all to Sylvia. I think we were both incredibly shy with each other. We both knew we enjoyed each other's company but that was not acknowledged. Yet it was at this time that I decided I wanted to marry her; so I took the old-fashioned course of seeking her father's consent to pay her my addresses. He told me that he and Mrs Patteson would be delighted to have me as their son-in-law; but there was one proviso. In view of her youth, she being just eighteen, we must wait till she was twenty-one before we got wed. To this I agreed without hesitation.

With this exciting secret in my heart, I did another crazy thing: I sought out a jeweller in Chichester and bought a second-hand diamond engagement ring. It wasn't then possible to buy new gold rings other than nine carat ones which looked like curtain rings. I was determined to get a ring that looked good and right; but my guess at the size of Sylvia's marriage finger was quite a bit out.

At the end of that month I was given three weeks' leave. I arranged to spend part of it with Sylvia at the home of her Uncle Robin and Aunt Molly in Forest Row in Sussex. We planned to meet at King's Cross Station and to cross London together to catch a train south from Victoria. It was in the taxi on that trip that I asked her to marry me and we exchanged our first kiss (not remotely resembling the examples we saw all the time on the screen in these days), and I tried to put the ring on her finger. Luckily it met with her approval but of course it had to go back to the jeweller to make it fit.

We got engaged on 4 April. A week later was my twenty-first birthday. For this occasion we'd organised a party at a pub in Horsham where my parents were staying in a cottage belonging to the Manor House, my old prep school. Sylvia was with us and I felt it was as much a celebration of our engagement as of my coming of age. It was also the first birthday I'd been able to celebrate with my family since my eighteenth.

Back with the squadron I was involved in two attempts to rescue Americans in their B17 Fortresses. On one of these missions I was able to spot an oil patch where a Fort had gone in and was able to summon help which came in the shape of two RAF rescue launches. The other mission was another of those uncomfortable ones, about which I have sometimes felt a bit guilty. I spotted the Fort I'd been sent out to bring home, flying due west down the centre of the English Channel. Were they intending to fly all the way home to America? I doubt it; indeed I can't imagine what was going on in the heads of the crew up there. Obviously they'd been badly roughed up by the Germans. Probably the captain of the ship was dead. Approaching from the north I got to within some eight hundred yards of them and then began doing steep turns to show them my profile. Their immediate reaction was to open fire on me. Carefully avoiding any direct approach, I circled at a distance and after each circle round them I headed off north for a minute and then came back to repeat the manoeuvre. Whenever I got within eight hundred yards they opened fire. I tried flying well above them and then a wee bit closer to them but always ready to shy away if their guns opened up again. After all such movements I headed homeward for a minute or a bit more before coming back to try again. They never changed course but went steadily on into the sunset, while I, seeing my fuel was getting low, decided I must leave them to their fate and fly home. I've no idea what happened to those Americans and have often wondered if there was anything more I could have done to bring them back to England.

My father's consecration as Bishop of Brechin was due to take place in St Paul's Cathedral, Dundee, on 2 May. I asked my CO if I could have enough leave to get up there and attend the ceremony. He told me not only that I could have two days' leave, but also that I could take a Spitfire and fly up to Leuchars, whence it was easy enough to get transport into Dundee. The plan was to fly up on the afternoon of the first and home on the morning of the third. But it was not to be. On 30 April I was told: 'Sorry, no Spitfire available. There's a bit of a flap coming up. But you can take the Tiger Moth.' Next day the wind blew at some forty to fifty miles per hour out of the north. Under those conditions it would have taken me a day and a half to get to Leuchars in the Tiger Moth against the hour and a half it would have taken in the Spit. With great regret the trip had to be cancelled; and I guess that was as much a disappointment to my family and to Sylvia as it was to me personally. She had travelled up to Dundee more to spend some time with me than to be present at the Consecration.

CHAPTER XVIII

Early in May I reached two landmarks: I got in my two hundredth hour of flying Spit XIIs and I completed a year's flying with 41 Squadron. As if to celebrate this double achievement I was sent on a solo mission to Ramsbury to join an air show, the purpose of which was to help the Royal Observer Corps in their task of identifying our own aircraft. After landing at Ramsbury I was directed to taxi along the grass edge of the field to an assembly point. The ground was extremely treacherous, verging on boggy; and I was afraid I might well get stuck in the mud. Feeling this drag on my undercarriage I opened up the engine and increased speed. A moment later my Spit tipped right up on its nose. That was not very good for it. Obviously I was unable to continue the exercise and I had to abandon my Spit and go home with my head hanging down. My own CO was sympathetic and would have taken no action against me. Later however I was to learn that higher powers thought I should be disciplined for my carelessness.

A week later I had the amazing experience of trying to shoot down (with cine-gun only of course) a Sunderland flying boat of Coastal Command. This was just about as hard as it was to deal with another Spitfire in a mock dogfight. The ability of this great flying boat to do steep turns was most surprising. My film recorded precious few hits in a 'fight' that lasted about a quarter of an hour.

On 16 May we were withdrawn from ops for a week to do some hard practice at air-to-air gunnery, cine-gun fighting and bombing. I don't think any Spitfire ever did much good with bombs. I note that my own average error when dive bombing was forty-eight yards on my best day. At my first attempt it was 120 yards. Low-level bombing was better; on my best day I actually averaged just a ten-yard error. At that distance a five hundred pound bomb might actually have destroyed the right target. In the middle of the course I was required to fly one Spit down to Bolt Head in Devon and bring a different one back. I imagine we were sussing out the place because as soon as our course was over the Squadron moved down there in readiness –

as we learned later – to cover the Normandy beaches during the Allied invasion of mainland Europe.

Bolt Head was a fascinating place. The airfield was simply a big grass field without runways, though the shape was such that there were two decent length strips on which one could take off or land. There was a sort of chain-mail spread over these strips which made the ground safe for flying even after heavy rain. The officers' mess was the Cottage Hotel at Hope Cove, some two miles from the airfield. The road between was a typical Devon country lane. We used to go up to the field by bus more often than not; and if we met any other traffic the other driver had to back until there was a field gate through which he could escape. Occasionally I made the trip by motor bike, which was a lot simpler. The hotel was great. I had a room with a beautiful view over the cove. It was possible to walk down to the little beach but not to swim since the beach was covered in a barbed wire entanglement – a relic from the days when invasion had been expected in the opposite direction.

We were barely settled in at Bolt Head when the order came through which posted me to Sheffield for a three-week disciplinary course – my punishment for tipping that Spit on its nose at Ramsbury. My CO was very cross about it but there was nothing he could do to prevent it. The totally maddening thing was that the Squadron was about to be given the task of covering the beachhead for the Normandy landings on 6 June.

The course was quite enjoyable and a big change from life with the squadron. It consisted almost entirely of marching about as we used to do at ITW under F/Sgt McTaggart. Though most of the course members were officers we all had to behave like airmen (i.e. ordinary aircraftsmen or 'erks') and treat the NCOs in charge of us with respect and obedience.

The local parish was Norton and I quickly found my way to the vicarage, where I shared my woes with the vicar, who was most kind and promptly invited Sylvia to come for a stay at the vicarage so that we could be together in what spare time I had. This made the posting almost as good as a period of leave, though I was glad enough to get back to the squadron at the end of it. This of course was because while dallying in Sheffield the invasion of France had begun and my colleagues were spending many hours flying over the battlefields and helping to make history.

The day after my return I flew as Blue 1 (Acting Flight Commander) for the first time. I think this was a deliberate move by my CO to indicate his displeasure at my having been removed from ops by higher powers at a time when we were all most needed. The actual mission was not a success: we'd flown over the French coast specifically to attack enemy shipping but failed to find any. We then flew further into France hoping to catch the odd enemy fighter but again with no joy.

One day about this time we were summoned to a squadron briefing. The CO told us that the powers that be wished to get shot of our MkXII Spits, since they were not building any more than the original one hundred and there soon wouldn't be enough of them to be viable for a frontline fighter squadron. So we were to undertake what some would see as a suicide mission: we were to dive bomb Cherbourg harbour. Of course, it would be OK to bale out but we were not going to be congratulated if we brought our aircraft safely back to base. While the ground crews were busy substituting five hundred-pound bombs for our usual thirty-gallon drop tanks the weather deteriorated. By the time we were due to take off aerial reconnaissance in the Cherbourg area showed that the port was completely covered by low cloud, so that dive bombing was out of the question. The mission was cancelled and to general relief never reinstated.

CHAPTER XIX

At the end of June a new phase in our work began: dealing with doodlebugs. The official German name for these weapons was V1, standing for Vergeltungswaffe 1 (Revenge weapon 1) later to be followed by the V2 rockets. Our official name for the V1 was 'Diver'. This was because of their habit of coming in at lowish altitude and then, when the engine stopped, tipping sharply and diving to the ground, where they would explode on impact. For the rest of my time with 41 Squadron our main defensive job was the anti-Diver patrol, while offensively the main task was to cover bombing raids on the launching sites from whence these ram-jet flying bombs were sent from France and the Low Countries towards London.

These German weapons were also known as terror weapons, and with some justification. I vividly recall hearing one for the first time as it came in over the coast at Friston. It was flying at about two hundred feet making this weird and frightening thumping sound. We knew that if the noise stopped it would mean that the bomb would come down. That didn't prevent the sound being highly alarming, though the silence that might follow would of course be worse.

Defending London from doodlebugs was done in three ways: first were the barrage balloons which were of course quite capable of downing the bombs but couldn't stop them from exploding on or near inhabited places; then there were anti-aircraft guns, which were given special zones in which to operate and in which it was more likely that the bombs would fall in open country; and finally came the fighters of ADGB (the Air Defence of Great Britain) of which 41 Squadron was a part. Our job was to patrol high up over the Channel and if possible to down the brutes into the sea. Often enough we had to follow our quarry a little inland but needed to keep careful note of where the anti-aircraft gunners had exclusive rights.

Most doodlebugs came in at between two hundred and two thousand feet and flew at some 370 mph. This was rather faster than our top speed at that height. The trick therefore was to spot them soon enough to use our great height advantage to dive down on them at over four hundred miles per hour in order to intercept the quarry while still having a speed advantage. Except in the unlikely event of coming at them from directly astern we needed also to judge how far ahead of the target to aim. This 'deflection' was of course necessary when firing at any moving target. It was to get used to this idea that part of our fighter training was that enjoyable sport – clay pigeon shooting.

Another technicality applied to all our shooting. Our two cannon and four machine guns were harmonised at two hundred yards. That meant that if pointed at a target two hundred yards away all the shells and bullets would hit it. A target further away would get a less intense, more scattered treatment as the bullets and shells, starting from guns spaced out over some fourteen feet of wing, dispersed to that same distance at four hundred yards; and the further off the target was after that, the less effective the fire would be. The lesson from all this is that the right range to open fire was exactly two hundred yards. Sometimes that was not practical but with flying bombs judiciously approached it was relatively easy.

We had for a while in our squadron a wild and foul-mouthed Aussie whose courage was outstanding but whose behaviour in the air was a menace to friend as well as foe. His theory was that you shouldn't open fire till you could see the whites of their eyes or rather when you could have seen them if the enemy was good enough to turn your way and not wear goggles. I don't know how he would have dealt with pilotless aircraft but guess he would have done the 'tip them over' trick which had been done successfully by one or two pilots but which was strictly forbidden as it was liable to do much damage to one's own aircraft. He died colliding with an ME109.

My own first success against doodlebugs came when I shot one down over the Kent countryside. Later it turned out that a Tempest pilot was claiming the same victory. I never actually noticed him at the time but had to accept that this was only a half success. Two days later I got another. That same day just before dusk, I and my Number Two were scrambled to try to deal with a doodlebug that had been spotted coming in while still some way out over the Channel. We didn't catch it and were then kept airborne for three-quarters of an hour and eventually were allowed to land only when it was raining and really dark. The Spitfire – and more particularly the MkXII – was not designed for night flying. The Griffon engine emitted great plumes of flame from its exhaust manifolds right in front of the pilot's eyes when he was trying to look along the nose on landing. In the daytime these flames were not a hazard but at night their light was spectacular and well-nigh blinding. So it was with some relief that we both got down safely at Friston, which was quite a small airfield.

On 11 July we moved to Lympne in Kent, where we really were in the doodlebug firing line. The Lympne airfield is another small one. Before the war it had been used exclusively by light civilian aircraft. There were no runways; the surface was simply mown grass. In order to get safely airborne in the limited space the Spit XII pilot had to rev up his engine, standing on the brakes and let go as soon as full throttle was achieved. That way with the maximum possible acceleration it was reasonably easy to get airborne within the airfield boundaries.

On one occasion I was about to do a test flight and having gone through the routine just described got rolling before I noticed that the boost gage was not registering. The power was certainly there, so that didn't seem all that important to me, though of course it was something to note for the test report. Much more alarming was a new factor about which I could do nothing, for it was now much too late to abort my takeoff. Even if I'd cut the engine there was no chance that I could stop inside the boundary. The new factor was that my air speed indicator was also not working; as I got airborne it registered my speed through the air as twenty miles per hour. When this happened I'd done over 370 hours' flying on Spitfires; that meant that I could make a reasonable guess at my true air speed; but to get it just right for landing was another matter. I thought I'd radio base and ask for suggestions but found the radio was out of order. I decided to fly the short distance to Manston, where there was a splendid long runway. There I simply flew down to ground level, touching down not in the normal stalling position but fully horizontal. That way I could close the throttle and let the 'plane take its own time to settle down onto the tail-wheel. I estimated that I touched down at about 150 instead of the usual ninety miles per hour. This whole flight only lasted ten minutes but they were quite the nastiest ten minutes I ever spent on a test flight. On reflection, I reckoned that it was safer to be a fighter pilot than a test pilot: a conclusion I certainly would not have reached had I been engaged in the Battle of Britain.

Lympne was ideally placed for a squadron engaged in intercepting dood-lebugs but unfortunately the weather turned very nasty as soon as we moved there and many of our chases failed because the quarry was in cloud and we had no way of getting at it. On one occasion however I had a clear view of an enormous flying bomb, at least twice the size of all those I'd seen hitherto. It was a lot slower than the usual type and I thought it should be easy enough to down it. Alas I failed. I fired all my ammunition into the thing and it just went on flying. I was also involved in five or six other fruitless chases but didn't get in range more than once in a three-week period; and that time my intended victim was downed by a Spit IX.

Having said that we were in the doodlebug firing line, I have to say that the vast majority of those we sighted passed harmlessly (as far as we were concerned) overhead. However no less than three actually landed on our airfield. Amazingly no one was killed but there were some narrow escapes. The first bomb exploded only a few yards from the officers' mess while I was playing a game of shove-halfpenny in the anteroom (our sitting room or perhaps drawing room as we'd call it in a private house as large as this). We all leapt to our feet and saw the massive plaster ceiling break away from one wall and begin to descend quite slowly until the whole thing was down, while we were all crowded against the wall opposite. We ended up very dirty but totally unharmed.

A few days later another doodlebug landed right on top of a house inhabited by a couple permanently stationed at Lympne. Ambulance and fire tender hastened to the scene, which was one of total devastation. The wall of the house that faced the airfield proper simply no longer existed; the place was a ruin. While searching through the rubble the rescue party heard a faint sound, which came not from within the ruined house but from the garden. In the garden there were a few bits and pieces belonging to the house but the only large object was an upside-down bath. It was from this that the faint sound had come. On turning the bath over, to the total astonishment of all present, was a somewhat bruised and battered but very much alive naked lady.

The last of the three hits on us was for me personally much the most frightening. I was waiting to take off with my Number Two close behind me when, as always, I checked that there was nobody coming in to land. This time however there was an aircraft on its approach. I didn't at first recognise it but began to get a bit worried when it seemed to be heading straight for me. I suppose it was about four hundred yards away when I realised it was a doodlebug with engine stopped doing its final dive. I was petrified. The thing just kept on coming straight for me and to this day I can't think why it didn't behave as doodlebugs usually did. Instead of hitting me it levelled off and passed just over my head, continuing a very gentle glide until it hit the ground some five hundred yards ahead of me, exploding and leaving a sizeable crater. I felt that had I been able to stand up in my cockpit I could have touched this lethal weapon as it passed. I dare say that in reality it was some ten feet above me. The crater was not in my way; so we then took off as planned and were soon patrolling in mid-Channel trying to knock some of the brutes down. Over July and August I clocked up a score of four doodlebugs destroyed.

It was some time about now that I suddenly became aware of something I'd never noticed before while all the commissioned officers of the squadron were drinking at the bar in the mess. Just occasionally I found the whole of my life on an operational fighter squadron very scary. No one else seemed to have any fear at all. While realistically I thought that my chances of survival were about even I didn't often let that worry me. In fact on more than one occasion I recall thinking, 'At least if I get killed my granny will be proud of me.' My comrades seemed to be universally chirpy. If one of them got killed, we would of course be sad. 'So and so's bought it over France,' we'd hear and then perhaps we'd drink to his future life – above, we hoped.

Back now to that evening at the bar: the curious thing I'd noticed, which I'd never observed before, was that every beer mug in every hand was shaking. Strange as it may seem this came as an enormous relief to me. 'If Pinky Glen has the jitters', I said to myself, 'then it's OK to be scared too.' Pinky Glen was our CO at the time and was our most distinguished pilot, winning two DSOs and two DFCs.

Early in August I had a fortnight's leave – in York for most of the time and then for a bit with Sylvia in Dundee. At the Pattesons' I met Sylvia's paternal grandmother, a marvellous old lady who had only just decided that she could no longer stand living in London where she'd been throughout the Blitz. The doodlebugs had been just too much for her. She never tired of telling me about them and her constant refrain was 'You've never *heard* such a noise.'

CHAPTER XX

Back on duty we were kept very busy, sometimes doing as many as five ops in a day. Most of these were defensive but we had an occasional treat, doing fighter sweeps over the battle area in France. It was on one of these that Tom Slack, my Flight Commander, was shot down. He managed to evade the Germans and got back home via Spain, but I personally never saw him again.

Soon after this the squadron was allowed to get thoroughly involved in the real war over France. Instead of our prime target being enemy fighters, which were now very rarely seen, we went out to destroy ground targets. We were especially interested in German transport – lorries on the roads and barges on the rivers. I notice, to my shame, that I described this mission as 'Great fun.' I probably wouldn't have done so had I known that just a week later I would be on the receiving end of the same sort of strafing. My Spit was twice hit by flak on this trip but the damage was not serious.

Normally the Spit XII was fitted with a thirty-gallon drop tank. This was fitted centrally between the two air intakes under the wings and it increased our endurance and hence our range by twenty-five per cent. Very rarely, this tank was replaced by a forty-five-gallon one. Obviously carrying this extra weight slowed us down a bit. When engaged in aerial combat we could jettison the tank, the fuel from which we always used before switching over to the main tank. On 27 August we were told to prepare for a special mission which required us to carry a ninety-gallon drop tank. This more than doubled our fuel load, so that in theory we could fly down to the Mediterranean.

Another strange bit of preparation we underwent was to try landing on a strip of runway marked out to resemble the flight deck of an aircraft carrier. This was quite hopeless: no matter how slowly we came in or how cleverly we stalled our aircraft on crossing the starting line or how violently we slammed on the brakes the moment we touched down, nobody got down in less than double the required distance.

I've heard that eventually some fighters did actually make the trip to the Med but can't believe that a Spitfire without arrester gear could possibly have landed safely on a carrier, still less a MkXII with the extra weight of the Griffon engine.

I suppose it was simply because these great ninety-gallon monstrosities had been built that the powers that be decided we should use them. With the extra ninety gallons of fuel and the extra drag of the tank it was only just possible to take off from a small airfield like Lympne. Once we were airborne we set out in the usual direction for France. Our job this time was to escort a vast number of Bostons, Havocs and Marauders which were engaged in a sort of shuttle service, bombing a German army in the Falaise Gap on the Seine. This was a big bend in the river, where the hapless Germans were caught by the advancing Allied troops and were being simply bombed to bits. It was an inferno over which we cruised up and down for an hour and a half, thanking God we were not down there.

All the time we were flying over this horror we never saw a single German aircraft. I had been longing to spot some enemy aerial activity, largely so that I'd got the excuse I needed to get rid of the ninety-gallon tank that was ruining the normal characteristics of my Spitfire. On this occasion there was hardly any flak to contend with either. Indeed the worst thing to afflict us was the aching backside that gradually came to dominate our feelings as we longed more and more to get out and fly home. In fact we were only airborne for two hours and ten minutes but it seemed much longer because of the rotten handling characteristics of our grossly overladen Spits.

On the thirtieth we had another glorious sweep over the Lille area. This time I was heavily involved in shooting up barges, six of which I damaged personally. There was a low ceiling (i.e. full cloud cover) below which we remained for about twenty minutes. I think we probably used up all our ammunition and in turn were attacked quite heavily by flak, though none of us got shot down and I personally got home unscathed.

On 1 September I got permission to do a rhubarb in the area of St Omer. There was one particular target that was to be our priority should we be lucky enough to spot it. It was any train that consisted of or contained long flat trucks carrying what would look like telegraph poles, which might possibly be covered up. At the time I'd no idea what these telegraph poles might be, but assumed they were some new nasty kind of weapon like the doodlebug. In fact, of course, they were V2 rockets, which the Germans had been setting up in Northern France and which they would be urgently desiring to get out of reach of the Allied armies now sweeping rapidly eastwards from Normandy.

I took off at dawn with my Number Two alongside me. We flew at sea level until we neared the French coast; then climbed to around five thousand feet to reconnoitre the territory. The roads were pretty deserted but very soon I saw the smoke of a train and headed that way to investigate. Sure enough, this was our priority target. In the train were eight of the flat trucks that had been described to us, each piled high with their 'telegraph poles'. Unfortunately there were not only trucks like these, but also an equal number of trucks which turned out to be flak wagons. I'm not sure of the numbers but my guess is that there were four anti-aircraft guns on each truck, making thirty-two guns in all. They were coupled up in pairs: two V2 wagons followed by two flak wagons, with a guard's van at the rear.

We'd had no specific instructions as to how best to immobilise a loco-motive. The safest course would be to approach it head on at ground level, for that way no guns could get me before I passed over the train. To my shame I didn't know enough about the anatomy of a French locomotive to know whether a frontal assault would have worked. In the end I decided to come in at tree-top height from the flank and aim at the driver's cab initially and spraying the engine forward from there. I think my attack was effective for as I passed over the engine there was a great explosion. It was however quite impossible to say what hit my Spit because all the guns on the train were blazing away at me. Everything seemed to be OK as I roared away but in a very short time my engine temperature began to soar, so that I knew I was losing glycol fast. Without this coolant my engine would seize up in a matter of minutes.

My Number Two was with me. I climbed steeply and headed north-west hoping I might be able to reach the sea, which I knew was swarming with the ships of the Royal Navy. It would, I thought, be easy enough to bale out over water and I'd soon be rescued. Stupidly I made no attempt to report back by radio, giving the map reference of the stopped train. Instead, when my engine seized up, I simply said 'Give my love to my true love and say I'll be all right.' I put the nose down to ensure I wouldn't stall and had time to trim the aircraft so that I was descending straight ahead. Then I undid my safety harness, pulled back the cockpit hood, rolled the Spit over and fell out.

I'd never practised parachuting but we'd all had a little bit of instruction as to how to do it. The main thing was to count up to three after leaving the aircraft before pulling the ripcord handle. After that one was supposed to be able to do a bit of steering by judicious pulling on the strings of the 'chute on the way down. That sounded fine in the calm of the lecture room but it didn't work like that when doing it for the first time for real. The moment I dropped clear I was grabbing frantically for that handle, which pulled easily enough, so that in no time I felt a violent jerk and looked up to see that gorgeous display of white silk umbrella which would allow me to drift safely down to earth. I also saw my beloved Spit seemingly stationary just above the 'chute and a lot too close to it for comfort. However all was well and gradually we parted company, the Spitfire diving more steeply and eventually crashing and bursting into flames.

After my panic had subsided I enjoyed for a few minutes the extraordinary silence and the beauty of the approaching landscape in the early morning light. All too soon, the problem of landing came upon me. I'd done absolutely nothing about steering; for there didn't seem any particular place to aim for even if I could have mastered the art of controlling the strings. However when about fifty feet from the ground I realised that I was moving pretty fast and headed straight for a large tree in the corner of a grass field. If I could just make a reasonable landing near there, I thought, I might be able to hide the 'chute and make a smart getaway.

I had no such luck. The 'chute caught on a branch of the tree and just as I thought I was going to make quite a good touchdown I was swung wildly upwards. The branch from which I was suspended broke and I fell heavily on my back onto a pile of stones at the foot of the tree. There was no hope of hiding anything, so I disengaged myself from my harness and ran for a gap I could see in the hedge around the field, hoping that at least I could get some distance from the 'chute before trying to hide somewhere.

I plunged through the gap to be confronted immediately by a Wehrmacht motorcycle combination. The driver was just getting off and promptly pointed his rifle in my direction. His companion in the sidecar manned a nasty-looking machine gun. The driver called 'Alt'. I 'alted. Then he came over and made a cursory examination of me to see if I carried a weapon, which I didn't. Strangely I remember feeling like laughing because I'd so often seen the exact picture of these Germans and their motor cycle combination in films. Somehow at first they hardly seemed real.

An even more unlikely scene opened up before me a few minutes later while one of my captors marched me into the nearby village of Esquelbeq. I suppose many of the locals had been observing my descent and they made as good preparation for me as had the Germans. As we neared the centre of the village, the population turned out as if for royalty, lined the street on both sides, waved little union flags and shouted, 'Vive l'Angleterre. Vive l'RAF' (letters pronounced in French of course).

Having arrived at the town hall, I had a brief interrogation by a German officer and was given my first taste of ersatz coffee, a peculiar drink like nothing I'd tasted before but welcome indeed as I was very thirsty, probably because I was afraid. I remembered to give the interrogator no information other than my name, rank and service number. He seemed rather at a loss as to what to do with me but eventually led me to a shop, above which was a sort of attic, where I was locked up and stayed for the whole day and the following night.

Next morning I was handed over to a Feldwebel (senior non-commissioned officer) whose job it would be to take me to Germany with his anti-aircraft gunners, who were retreating without their guns. There were quite a lot of them and they travelled in four trucks. I was in the leading one with the Feldwebel; my watch, cigarette case, lighter and wallet were in one of the other trucks. We formed just the sort of group that 41 Squadron had enjoyed strafing a day or two before. I had mixed feelings when, very soon after we set out, we ourselves became the target of Allied planes. I think they were Mustangs. Between them they carried both guns and bombs and they did a remarkable job. Two of our trucks were knocked out, several Germans were killed; one who leapt into the ditch just about tore his thumb off in the process. The truck that carried my valuables was obliterated but nobody in the leading truck was hurt.

I remember feeling that I might be going to be rather unpopular with my captors after this incident. In fact it made no difference at all. My German was quite adequate for the purpose of conversing with them and before long the Feldwebel and I were usually engaged in deep conversation. He told me he'd been a theological student when war broke out, and like all good Christians was strongly anti-Nazi. He had of course been conscripted into the Wehrmacht. He told me that they all knew the war was as good as over. 'Deutschland kaput. Alles kaput.' was the sort of thing they were all saying; in other words, 'We've had it.' He however was absolutely certain it was now right for all Germans to fight to defend the Fatherland.

This journey was particularly exciting because we were all aware of the fluid nature of the frontline. At one point we had to do a hasty about turn and divert to the south. The news was that the Americans were in the town immediately ahead of us. That was General Patton and his tanks. About this time I was left alone for a few moments while we were all stationary.

I wondered whether at this point I should have a go at escaping. If I could just hide for a few minutes they'd surely go on without me considering their great need for haste and, as I thought, the total unimportance of their prisoner. I looked out trying to gauge my chances. By the time I'd decided they were about nil the Feldwebel was back in the truck. His first words were 'If you are thinking about escaping I beg you not to try it. It would be my bounden duty to shoot you, my friend. You might also like to know that I am one of the best shots in the German army.'

CHAPTER XXI

Although we'd been on the road all day we made slow progress if measured by our nearness to Germany. In the evening of 2 September we arrived in Brugge, one of the loveliest towns in Europe, though I was quite unaware of that at the time. All I knew was that we were somewhere in Belgium. I was taken to a grim stone building which was clearly the local HQ of the German army. There I was questioned by a smart senior officer, who – I suspect – was not supposed to be questioning me at all. In any case I only gave him the standard answers, just my name, rank and service number. I was given a slice of their black bread with margarine and a bowl of soup and was then thrust into a dungeon for the night.

And what a night that was! Once the door had been shut on me and locked and bolts rammed home as well, I was left in total darkness. I'd just had time to see that the floor consisted of damp cobbles and that there was a straw palliasse to lie on. The walls were all wet and dripped gently all through the night. Outside the door there was the occasional sound of marching feet. I reckoned that in the exceedingly unlikely event of my being able to open the door I'd still be faced with an armed sentry in the passage. I suppose I should have felt flattered that they thought they had to take such elaborate precautions to prevent my escape.

The main trouble was the cold. I was reasonably warmly dressed, having taken off from Lympne in the cool of the early morning; but this place felt as if it could never have been warm in a thousand years. I crept onto the palliasse and tried to sleep but to no avail. After two or three hours I began to think I might freeze to death; so I wriggled about and tried to see if I could get any warmer by lying under rather than on top of the straw. I don't think it would actually have been any improvement but just to move a bit did seem sensible. The trouble was that the sentry outside the door had other ideas. There came a great racket as the bolts were drawn back and the lock undone. The squeaking door opened and in staggered the sentry obviously very drunk and very dangerous. He told me in barely intelligible German to get against the wall and hold my hands up. 'You were trying to escape', he said, 'and I'm going to shoot you.' He then ordered me to turn around with my back to him. I obeyed. Next he shoved the muzzle of his rifle into the small of my back and asked me if I could think of any possible reason why he shouldn't kill me.

I've often wondered since then what would have happened if I'd not had a reasonable understanding of German. As it was I talked on and on as if my life depended on keeping talking, as indeed I felt it did. I remember telling him that I'd met his commanding officer and that he was a real gentleman and an officer of the old type who wouldn't stand for any indiscipline in his soldiers. I told him that if he were to shoot me his CO would almost certainly have him shot. I told him there was no way I could possibly attempt to escape from this dungeon without tools or any help from outside. I told him people did stupid things when they were under the influence of alcohol. I told him that if he shot me he would be a war criminal and that Germany would shortly be beaten and he'd better be good to me now. I can't remember all I said but know I kept it up for what seemed an age. All the time he'd got his gun stuck hard into the small of my back and I could imagine his finger on the trigger. Several times he interrupted my flow to reiterate his accusation that I was trying to escape. He seemed not to take in what I was telling him. Now and then he'd push hard with the rifle into my back, which was already uncomfortable as a result of my bad parachute landing, so that I was in quite severe pain.

In the end, after what seemed like an eternity or at least twenty minutes but which was probably not much more than five, he took his gun away from my back, walked out of the door, and locked and bolted it behind him. I collapsed like a jelly to the floor, filled with a massive sense of shame rather than relief. For me this was a nightmare scene that haunted me for many years after. Of course, I'd already come to terms with my ongoing anxiety and thought I'd got that under pretty good control. This was different altogether. This was sheer terror. This, I felt then, was abject cowardice. I thought I now understood the words of the psalmist who wrote: 'I am a worm, and no man: a very scorn of men, and the out-cast of the people.'

Eventually I dragged myself back to my straw palliasse and even managed some snatches of sleep before the door was again opened and a soldier I'd not seen before told me to get up and follow him. I was taken to a normal daylit room and given some breakfast – more black bread and margarine and a cup of ersatz coffee – which was most welcome. Shortly after this I was taken outside and handed over to the anti-aircraft gunners who'd brought me thus far. Now they were to complete their journey and take me into Germany. I greeted the Feldwebel like a long lost friend!

We had an uneventful journey to Dusseldorf, arriving in the late afternoon. The Feldwebel asked me if I'd like to stay the night with a civilian in a normal home. This I could do if I'd give my parole not to escape but be ready to journey on with the gunners next morning. To this I readily agreed and was taken to a little house, where I was greeted by a kindly woman who turned out to be a widow with one son who was fighting on the Eastern Front. She gave me a wonderful meal and talked at length about her son and her anxieties about him, which were all too natural; the war with the Soviet Union was a far more murderous affair than the relatively genteel fighting in the West.

I had a hot bath – an almost unbelievable luxury – and went to bed in a very pretty room with a crucifix above my head. This lovely hostess was clearly a devout Catholic. When I was in bed she knocked on the door, came in and sat beside me. We went on talking for about an hour. I felt my German was beginning to get quite good by now and the conversation went easily and most enjoyably. Finally she stooped over and kissed me goodnight!

Next morning the Feldwebel turned up on the doorstep to reclaim his prisoner. Accompanied by just one other soldier we went to the railway station and boarded a train for Frankfurt am Main. I had withdrawn my parole by now but realistically did not expect to get any chance of escaping until, after alighting at Frankfurt, my guards, moving swiftly through a dense crowd of people, got a yard ahead of me; whereupon I turned about and walked as fast as I could back the way we'd come. I nipped up a bridge and came down on a different platform. I sat down on a bench and tried to think what my next move should be. I was of course still wearing my RAF uniform with my wings and rank insignia and imagined everyone seeing me would know that I was a POW. I decided the only sensible thing to do would be to find a goods train, get on it and remove my tunic and perhaps turn it inside out. I'd just made this decision when a woman sat down beside me and asked if I were in the Luftwaffe. 'Yes,' I said, 'I'm a fighter pilot.' We chatted for a few minutes. Then I told her I must be off and made my way back to the bridge, intending to see from that vantage point if there were a suitable goods train in the station. At the top of the steps who should meet me but my escort! I was amazed that they didn't seem in the least perturbed by my ten-minute-long escape from their custody.

We hadn't a train to catch. I was marched some mile or so and delivered to a camp which I was to learn was known as 'Dulagluft'.

Dulagluft was in fact the interrogation centre for all 'enemy' aircrews. This was the place where the interrogators knew their stuff. The procedure was quite different from any questioning I'd experienced hitherto. Immediately on arrival I was asked the usual questions and gave the usual answers. When I would not tell them my squadron I was taken to a room and locked in. Here I stayed in solitary confinement for five days. There were no washing facilities. Food was restricted to one slab of bread and margarine and a small bowl of soup, plonked on the floor once a day. Twice a day I was allowed to go under escort to the toilet block, where I was issued with two small sheets of toilet paper for the first visit; then no more until next day. After five days I was very tired, very dirty and very hungry.

Then out of the blue everything changed. I was brought some clean underwear, given some soap and taken to a bathroom and allowed to have a good wash. After this I was led into a very pleasant room, which to my consternation had '41' printed on a card stuck onto the outside of the door.

Within was a man in the uniform of a Wehrmacht major. He invited me to sit down, offered me fruit from a large bowl on the table between us and a choice of cigar or cigarette when I had gratefully eaten.

It had of course been dinned into us that we should answer no questions beyond name, rank and number, but what if the question were 'Would you like an orange?' Surely it was OK to say 'yes' to that?

Then he said, 'Have you been treated all right since you got here?'

To this I certainly said I'd been treated abominably.

'That must have been a terrible mistake', he said – all this in impeccable English. I continued to converse with him on matters that I was sure had no significance whatsoever. Then he suddenly said 'We know you were flying a Tempest.' This being untrue as well as unexpected caught me on the hop. I think my reply was 'Oh, yes?'

Next he said that he needed to be sure I was a genuine RAF pilot and not a spy. Once the truth was established they would be able to inform the Red Cross who would see to it that my next of kin was informed of my safety. To this end he needed the answers to just a few harmless questions such as the name of my squadron commander. He went on to point out that he himself was a very gentle person but if he didn't get the information he had to have then there was always the SS to whom he might be obliged to hand me over. He was sure I was aware that they had a reputation for ruthlessness that was not altogether undeserved. I wasn't fooled by that line but perhaps I was by what followed. I was certainly immensely relieved when he stopped asking me questions to which the answers were obviously not for me to give.

He then started talking about matters political. His particular subject was the iniquities of Stalin's Soviet Union and the absurdity of Britain being allied to this tyranny. I think I remained non-committal but certainly not silent – as I should have been. In the end it became clear that what he really wanted to know was what chance I thought there was of making peace between Britain and Germany so that they could then together fight against the Communist menace from the East. To this I know I was not non-committal but laughed out loud. I gave him my very firm view that we (and incidentally of course the Americans) would continue the war with Germany until it was won. Reflecting on this exchange I felt very guilty. On the other hand looking back long afterwards I can't believe my disobedience to instructions did anything to harm our war effort.

Back in my cell I was no longer treated to the starvation and dirt regime but that night there was a fearsome air raid, about which we heard the details next day. It seems this was the first thousand-bomber raid by the RAF. It seemed to go on for most of the night. We remained locked in our cells while our guards were down below in the air raid shelter. One Lancaster crashed almost on top of the camp and every few minutes I was sure my end had come. I remember feeling how strange a fate it would be to be wiped out by our own bombers after progressing in safety thus far. It was a terrifying ordeal; yet with one part of my mind I was rejoicing that we'd so thoroughly turned the tables on our enemies.

The day after this, in spite of a threat to hold me in Dulagluft indefinitely, I was suddenly told to get ready to leave and a couple of minutes later I was being marched to the railway station. Then began the most uncomfortable journey of my life. There were ten of us packed into one small compartment. We were on the train for five days and nights without a break. We took turns to lie on the luggage racks, allowing eight others to sit in tolerable comfort on the seats. Sleep was very difficult. The train kept starting and stopping and did most of its forward progress by night.

Eventually we arrived at Barth, a small town on the Baltic Coast between Stettin and Stralsund. From the station we were marched to our prison camp, known as Stalag Luft 1. Here we got installed in our huts, ten to a room where we had five double (one above the other) bunks with wooden slats and palliasses to lie on and reasonably warm blankets, which would soon become important.

The terrain was simply sand. In the distance to the north there were fir trees and beyond them the North Sea. We soon learned about the tunnelling activities that had been in progress for a long time. Just as we arrived at the camp the order had come through from Britain that no more escapes were to be attempted. This was because of the tragic events surrounding the mass escape from Stalag Luft 3 at Sagan. Most of those escapees were caught and murdered. To escape at this stage of the war and in face of that murderous German policy was clearly absurd; but to pretend to be planning to escape was still legitimate; so the tunnelling went on though always stopping short of the perimeter fence. One marvellous project in which I was not personally involved was planned in view of the regular tour round the camp by a steam roller. This used to puff round between the warning wire and the perimeter fence so regularly that watches could be set by its progress. The plan was to dig several converging tunnels all leading to a large pit beneath the path of the steamroller. The actual pit was only begun the moment the roller had passed that point. Next time round, the pit having been evacuated, the machine fell in exactly as planned. I can't remember if it was ever removed. The whole thing happened out of my own range of vision. I do know that the circumnavigation of the camp ceased. Perhaps by this time the Germans knew we were not going to be tunnelling under the perimeter fence any more.

The camp was vast. It contained at that time about ten thousand Americans, 2,500 RAF aircrew and a few Russians who were not air force but army prisoners and who were treated like dirt by the Germans. Towards us they behaved for the most part with correctness and even kindness in some instances.

I soon began to feel very sorry for our guards who seemed to grow older and more miserable each week. By the end of the war they were almost all members of the Volkssturm – the equivalent of our Home Guard. Few of them looked under seventy. Officially we had no dealings with them except through our appointed traders, who were able to make the most amazing deals such as a radio valve for a bar of soap. After soap, the most highly prized item was – for the goons (our name for our guards) – cigarettes, of which we always had an abundance.

The food supplied by the Germans was meagre but probably not at first much less or worse than they had themselves. The great difference, which made us better off by far than our goons, was the American Red Cross parcels which every single one of us received every week until mid-December. Apart from the splendid food, which included a marvellous and very substantial piece of chocolate called a D bar, each parcel also contained a thousand cigarettes. I was a heavy smoker but even I couldn't get through more than 350 a week. The result of this nicotine largesse was that we all had great stores of fags which were used more as currency than for smoking.

One of my great joys was that I met up here with Herbert Wagner, an American member of 41 Squadron, who was as keen on bridge as I was, so that we quickly became partners and soon worked out a highly complicated system of conventions which I wrote out in full in a booklet we made available to anyone who wished to play with us. We played for one fag a hundred, which was virtually meaningless. Long before our release the fags in use consisted of little more than empty tubes of cigarette paper. To get some idea of the relative value of things, long before the end came one D bar was changing hands for two thousand cigarettes. Although we were pretty regular winners in the nine-thousand-odd rubbers of bridge we played together, I doubt if we earned the price of a D bar in the eight and a half months of playing for some eight hours a day.

Apart from bridge my main occupation was translating the German news bulletins into English for the benefit of the lot of us. This was an interesting job since it often turned out that the German news was a good deal more accurate and up to date than that of the BBC, to which a clandestine ear was always tuned and which was secretly distributed by word of mouth only to each room, whereas my version was down in writing for all to see. Having this job also got me in close and friendly touch with the camp education officer, Dr Karlheinz Steinhauer, to whom I gave my parole so that we could go for walks outside the camp and polish up my German.

CHAPTER XXII

On arrival at the camp I had an examination by a doctor who tidied up my still wounded back, though, unsurprisingly, he didn't get me X-rayed. The fact that I had a dislocated spine was not discovered for several years. It continued to trouble me from time to time but it was seldom worse than mildly uncomfortable.

On the spiritual front I felt greatly deprived. All through my RAF time I'd been able to get fairly regularly to Communion and I'd continued to enjoy an active and mystical prayer life. Now I felt a great need of a confessor and of my sacramental communion. We had to begin with no Anglican priest. There were two chaplains, a Presbyterian and a Roman Catholic. Both ran regular Sunday services and I went to both of them. Although the Presbyterian did have the occasional Communion service, which I joined in, it felt so strange to me that I passed up the opportunity to partake of the Sacrament. I went to see the Catholic priest and asked him if he would hear my confession. He said he would of course be happy to provided I first agreed to submit to Rome. I had not the slightest intention of doing that so I then asked him if he could give me Communion in the special circumstances in which we found ourselves. His reply was a firm negative.

It wasn't until January that an Anglican chaplain arrived in our camp, by which time I'd more or less appointed myself to that office, gathering a few like-minded people together for a short spell of daily prayer. Now we had a priest I found I had to instruct him in the art of hearing confessions. I also acted as server when he presided at Communion for the tiny gathering of Anglicans who were sufficiently interested to join us. Keeping water unfrozen, begging wine off the German authorities and parting with a bit of my meagre ration of bread was all part of my office.

One other totally useless project of mine was in fact a source of considerable pride to me. I spent long hours – indeed almost all the time I was neither dealing with the news or playing bridge – in building a system for making gas in order to supply our room with light for the frequent occasions when the electricity supply was cut off. This entailed first of all making the tools and then using tins that had come with Klim, our dried milk, in the Red Cross parcels, to create the pipework and condenser necessary for the system. It worked. We got a light equivalent to about two candles at the cost of a small briquette of coal We used it on perhaps three occasions before the fuel shortage became so acute that it was resolved that all our fuel must go to heat rather than light. We could do without seeing each other for a while and freezing to death seemed a real possibility.

On the whole we didn't have too bad a time up until Christmas, when the last entertainment took place and a genuine bit of good cheer was had by most of us. We always had the problem of isolation from our homes. I never received a letter or card during my eight and a half months as a POW. Then almost immediately after Christmas things took a turn for the very much worse. Red Cross parcels stopped coming. The German food ration was drastically cut and winter became an ordeal such as few if any of us had ever experienced The temperature dropped to minus thirty degrees Celsius. Fuel supplies were so low that we dared not burn more than three briquettes a day. By the end of February the last of the Red Cross parcels that had been wisely hoarded were finished – apart of course from the great store of cigarettes. For our last six weeks in the camp our food ration was one loaf of bread and one ounce of margarine a week plus sometimes some very watery soup. We still got a bit of ersatz coffee or tea and the bread was that wonderfully sustaining black loaf, which I found I could cut into thirty-five slices and thus give myself five meals a day, the last of which would have margarine as well as my wafer of bread.

Mentally life was tough for all of us and by the end there were a thousand men locked up in the psychiatric block, at least temporarily round the bend, as we termed any mental disorder. Towards the end we were too weak to take violent exercise but we could, and most of us did, exercise our minds. We had a good library, including one book of some two hundred pages called *Discards at Contract Bridge*, which I read through several times from cover to cover. How to cope with the increasing cold and hunger was the biggest problem, to which there were no perfect solutions. Some of the weirdest stratagems were digging up old potato peelings, which in palmier days we had carelessly dumped, stalking – for days on end – and eventually catching, killing, skinning and eating a wretchedly thin cat and chewing, even occasionally swallowing, small portions of leather belt. We could dream about bacon and eggs; I often did; but to talk about them was taboo.

Before our hunger reached that acute phase and when the temperature had sunk to near its lowest point it was decided to build a skating rink. The way this was done was to build a sand wall about two inches high all round the area we'd planned to use and then to bring buckets of water from the ablutions (bathrooms without baths) and just tip them out on the ground. At the time there was no rationing of water and, with plenty of people helping, the job was eventually accomplished. As each bucket was tipped onto the frozen ground the water, already very near freezing point actually froze solid. This meant that instead of a smooth sheet of ice what we got was a great number of little ice hillocks. Of course if the sand had not been so cold the whole project would have been unthinkable as the water would simply have disappeared into the ground as soon as it made contact. In the event it all worked very well for a few days, although on the first day the rink was quite unusable. The day after however the sun shone brightly enough to begin to melt the ice hillocks and to give us an almost smooth rink. There were quite a lot of skating boots in the camp and I managed to borrow a pair and do a bit of wobbly skating myself. A day or three later we had an even sunnier time and the rink vanished. There was talk of reinstating it but the energy was not available.

In our RAF portion of the camp we had three deaths. The first was a shooting by one of the guards, one of the few really virulent Nazis. He was technically justified, though I doubt if any of the other guards would have done it. The prisoner concerned stepped over the warning wire which was fixed some ten feet inside the perimeter fence. This was strictly forbidden and we all knew how dangerous it was to do this. He simply wanted to retrieve a football a couple of yards beyond his reach from the right side of the wire. He was shot dead. The next was someone who just collapsed and died from starvation. My guess is that he had by this time a weak heart but we all felt that it might happen to any of us. The third was the most crazy and tragic of them all: he died of overeating.

How that came about was all tied up with a change in the German command. A new camp commandant arrived about a week before our liberation. His job was clearly to be nice to the prisoners. His first act was to discover and produce for us the ten thousand Red Cross parcels that had been lying at the railway station for the last month or two. Before these were delivered to us in our huts the medical officer came round to every room and gave us a severe warning about the dangers of eating too much or anything that we'd tried to cook and then found unpalatable. For my part this was quite unnecessary: I couldn't eat more than a few mouthfuls when the new plenty was there in front of me. Most of us felt much the same. However in one room they made a cake. When it was cut into ten slices and everyone had tried it, nine of them said they couldn't eat it; it didn't seem right. The tenth man ate the lot, was violently ill and died the same day.

I'm not sure how near we came to having a fourth and more horrific death – by lynching. Someone was caught stealing a fellow prisoner's food. The situation was ugly and only good basic discipline and the good sense of the senior British officer prevented the catastrophe that might have followed. He got the culprit away and organised with the German Commandant that, for his own safety, this man should be placed in solitary confinement until the end of the war.

When the Russian armies were clearly going to be with us in a few days the senior Allied officers went to see the Commandant about the forthcoming evacuation by his guards. There had been talk about marching us to the west as the Russians approached from the east. Thankfully nothing came of this and our senior officers were informed that they could take over the camp next day after the Germans had pulled out. 'OK,' they replied, 'but you will leave your transport behind; we shall need it.'

'That's going too far', said the Commandant. 'We still have the guns and we'll be taking our transport with us.' But they didn't. When they tried none of the vehicles would start for none had a distributor arm, nor were spares available. So the poor devils marched out and for a day we were in sole possession of everything in the camp and in the surrounding area. A small party was sent out to take over the local airfield, which was accomplished with no opposition.

There were many dead Germans about and a few live ones too. The saddest sight was a family piled up, all shot. It was presumed the father had shot the others then turned the gun on himself. We were told that this was a widespread occurrence because Joseph Goebbels had told the German people that if the Russians came they would be barbarians who would rape, loot, and kill and spare no one.

I dare say there was an element of truth in this but our own experience was very different. We were liberated by Marshal Rokosovsky and his crack troops, who did indeed despoil the local farmers in order to bring us food, but who struck us as a well-disciplined and professional group of soldiers. They were most friendly to us, teaching us some basic Russian and learning a word or two of English. Two long days later we drove ourselves to the airfield and took off in an American B17 for England.

CHAPTER XXIII

The flight was memorable in several ways. Obviously to be going home was immensely thrilling. The American captain of the ship was a humorous fellow who informed us that we would be landing at Ford in Sussex and that he'd never landed a Fortress in the dark before but was going to have to now. The 'plane was packed with men. My own position was right in the nose of the machine, so that I had a wonderful forward view but would also be the first person to get wiped out if we ran into a hard object at the end of the runway when we came in to land. In fact the flight went perfectly and the landing couldn't have been better executed. I did have all the same a slightly uneasy feeling as we neared the end of the runway, still travelling at a tidy speed. In next to no time we'd left the runway and taxied to the place where we were to disembark. It was explained to us that we had to go immediately to be deloused. This was a reasonably speedy business, after which feeling clean but almost unreal I was free to telephone Sylvia and my parents.

I got through to Sylvia at once. After almost nine months without a word from her I think our conversation was a bit stilted. She was almost lost for words and I wasn't much better. However I did say 'Let's get married on Saturday week.' I'd not thought out at all what this might mean to our parents. I just took it for granted that if Sylvia were happy about the idea all would be well. And she was. And it was. So far from reminding us that we'd promised to wait until she was twenty-one, C.P. – as all his friends called my father-in-law to be – organised the licence (no time for Banns) and agreed to tie the knot in his church of St Sampson, York. The ceremony was fixed for 9 a.m. on Saturday, 26 May, just ten days after I'd left Germany. My own father said he would be delighted to share in the wedding and in the end it was fixed that C.P. presided over the wedding proper while my father celebrated a nuptial Eucharist.

I'd been given a month's leave, which gave us time to plan not only the wedding, but also the honeymoon. Stupidly we relied on advice from our elders and ended up going to the Old Red Lion at Stow-on-the-Wold, of which a bit more a bit later. My parents had stayed there and been well satisfied.

Their judgement was not only a bit out in that respect, but also in what they should give me to eat. I'd weighed fourteen stone on 1 September in the previous year but was now just seven stone; but I'd ceased to be hungry. All those dreams of bacon and eggs didn't make me capable of consuming much at all, certainly not the lashings of good food my parents at first set before me. Britain was still strictly rationed for food and other things too, like furniture. I had been given, like all ex-POWs, two ration books so that I could have twice as much of all the precious rationed food as anyone else. It took me about ten to twelve days to begin to want to use all that bounty.

I returned to York on 25 May and after spending what was left of the day with the Pattesons repaired to the deanery for the night. The Dean was Eric Milner-White, who had been Dean of King's when I sat for my Cambridge scholarship and who was a great friend of Michael Peck and other friends of mine. He had generously offered to put me up since it was not done for a bridegroom to spend the night before the wedding under the same roof as his bride. We had fifteen wedding guests, including amazingly David and Dorothy Dewing, through whom in a way we had first got to meet each other.

Sylvia had concocted a wonderful white lace wedding dress while I had not to worry at all about clothes as I could be married in the uniform of a F/O in the RAF.

The wedding was a highly emotional affair for ourselves and our families. I was in a sort of dream throughout but awake enough to see tears coursing down my father's face, a sight which I'd never seen before. I've no doubt that the pain suffered by Sylvia and all our parents was greater than anything I'd had to bear, apart perhaps from the episode in the dungeon at Brugge, which haunted me for the next thirty years. A new factor in my understanding of my parents' pain was that I learned about my brother John's going missing just a couple of months after the report from the Red Cross that all was well with me.

It was infuriating that all that funny business in Dulagluft was supposed to ensure that the Red Cross would be informed of my safety in the hands of the Germans. Yet the first anyone in Britain knew about it was when my first letter reached Sylvia three months after I'd gone missing. Meanwhile my father, during a conference in Edinburgh, was faced with a young cleric who told him he'd been asked to pass on a message from the Air Ministry.

'But you don't have to worry,' he said, 'they've obviously made a mistake and you know all about this already. It's only about your son John going missing.' That in fact meant that two of his sons had gone missing and once again the news came from the Air Ministry without any assurance of his son's survival. My mother was always expecting the news that I was dead or if not dead at least horribly disfigured – probably by fire. Sylvia's parents were desperately worried that such might well be the case. Sylvia however was almost always sure that I was alive and would come home to her.

John had baled out over Italy. He'd made a better job of it than I had. He evaded capture, though the farmhouse he went to for shelter turned out to be the only one of the three he saw before him that was not occupied by the Germans. He was kept hidden for some time – long enough to begin to learn the language and was eventually brought home via a rowing boat and a Royal Navy submarine, making rendezvous in the Adriatic.

Wedding presents were even more of a problem then than they are today because the shops were so bare. In the event we got far more by way of cheques than anything else. In all we received over £200. I'd always managed to save money and one enormous benefit from having been in a POW camp was that I received back-pay plus hard-lying allowances which together came to almost £1,000. When we set off for our honeymoon we had very nearly enough money to buy the sort of house we wanted. I was firmly of the opinion that we shouldn't borrow money even for buying a house. The game of Monopoly had taught me to hate the idea of mortgaging any of my property!

When the wedding breakfast was over, our presents opened and our guests departed, we took a taxi to the station and set off for London. The train was packed and for the first part of the journey we were compelled to stand in the corridor or sit on our suitcases. We then went to Greenford Rectory where we spent our wedding night. I suppose the most unusual aspect of this was that before we went to bed we suggested to Donald Harris, our host, that he might give us one of his pre-wedding talks since neither of our parents had done the usual in this respect. Donald obliged but I'm not sure that either of us got much out of it. For me the best part of that night was simply admiring Sylvia in the bath. This was the first time we'd seen each other totally unclothed and I vividly remember feeling awe and wonder before the beauty of my wife.

Next day we went to pick up the car which my generous aunt Christian had given us when she entered the religious community of the Holy Name. She had left it with her friend, Sylvia Fletcher-Moulton, who soon became our friend too. We drove the car to Stow-on-the-Wold and booked in at the Old Red Lion, whose proprietor was a clergyman who had left the job and preferred secular employment; as had the local garage boss, who let us down equally badly. These two gentlemen certainly did nothing to enhance the status of the clergy in my eyes. The hotel took temporary possession of Sylvia's ration book and my two; so we looked forward to some good food in adequate quantities. I suppose it was a bit better than I'd had in Germany but that's about all I could say for it. Every course of every meal was skimpy and dull, the worst being the so-called soup, which seemed always to consist of Marmite in hot water. Having been quite unable to eat a decent meal when I first got home I now felt perpetually hungry; so it was most frustrating to be given meals which might well have satisfied an old-age pensioner but which were wholly inadequate for me. The fact that the hotel had my two ration books made not the least difference to the niggardly diet they provided; yet this was an establishment that had been commended by relations of both of us.

We were quite happy to see the back of Stow. Its baleful effect on us was however not yet over. On our way there we'd got a puncture, so I'd dropped the spare wheel off at the local garage and said we'd pick it up when we left as there was no desperate hurry for it. When we did leave we picked up the tyre, stowed it in the boot, paid the bill and departed. A month or so later we managed to get another puncture. On fitting the spare wheel – would you believe it? – I found that its tyre was still as punctured as it had been when we left it at the Stow garage.

From Stow we drove to York and on arriving at the home of my parents-in-law I conceived the ridiculous notion that it would be a good idea to lift my bride over the threshold. Had I tried such a thing a year earlier I dare say it would have come off quite well; but now I was a shade lighter in weight than my wife and nothing like as strong. My back simply gave way and I was in quite a bit of pain. At this time I'd no idea that my back was still in trouble due to my baling out. I was soon back at Cosford, where I underwent what was called a rehabilitation course. I remember nothing about it except that at the end of it I was declared to be A1 – perfectly fit. I knew I wasn't; but I was determined to get on with my life and, if needed, go back to war, for we were still fighting the Japanese in the Far East.

That proved unnecessary and I was sent off on leave again for another month, which was twice extended and became more or less indefinite. We decided to have a second try at a honeymoon that might be more of a success. Michael Peck had by this time bought from Eastick's Yacht Station at Acle his and our favourite Broads sailing boat, *Moss Rose*, and very generously and trustingly lent her to us as his wedding present. So early on 6 August we went to Acle to pick up the boat and go sailing. We'd taken a few odds and ends with us, including a bit of food, but had intended to stock up on our way to Acle or at a local shop.

We had not bargained for the atom bomb and the end of the war in the Far East. VJ day found us with no shops open and just one old man at the yacht station. At least he was able to let us take *Moss Rose*, which we did with some trepidation. Sylvia had never sailed before and we were faced with a very strong wind and a rusty captain as well as a novice crew, who had just discovered she was pregnant.

We'd not sailed more than about one hundred yards when the jib was torn from top to bottom by the sheer strength of the wind. We moored for the night and I went back to the yacht station and was delighted to find they had a spare sail that I could buy and use to replace our ruined jib. Next day dawned bright and breezy – just perfect weather for sailing. We sailed all day, covering some thirty-five miles of river. It was really far too much for Sylvia; I was certainly not being a good husband but a very selfish one, as I persisted in keeping going long after she was feeling stressed out. At last we moored in a lovely spot just inside one of the Broads. We had a meal and then a long night's rest followed by a whole day of almost total inactivity. The sun shone brightly and there wasn't a breath of wind to tempt me to get sailing again.

When we finally resumed our sailing I took it much more gently and we did no very long sails. Our relationship improved so that in the end we found it a mostly enjoyable as well as a useful experience. We were still getting to know each other, strange as that may sound for a couple who'd been engaged for sixteen months and married for nearly three.

With the approach of September I wrote again to Harold Layton and asked if he'd like me back at the Manor House for another term. He said yes, being still very short of staff. Mrs Lattey, who was a great friend of the school and who had had two sons there, invited Sylvia and me to stay with her, which we did. This time my youngest brother, Martin, was just starting his final year at prep school; so once more I found a younger brother calling me 'Sir'. He wasn't quite as punctilious as Stephen had been and I'm sure he never addressed me with such respect in the holidays. I enjoyed the teaching I did and became sure that what I wanted to do eventually was to be a schoolmaster.

The author's childhood home

The author with his parents, siblings and pets in
Cuddesdon in the summer before the war

The author's grand-
father, General
Buckle

Charlie van Goens, who, flying as my No.2, was shot down by our own
AA guns and killed in August 1944

The author, Tangmere 1944

OC 'B' Flight 41 Sqn, Pinky Glen DSO and Bar, DFC and Bar, in the early days as our Flight Cdr with just one DFC

Gizzie, F/LT Lord Guisborough

Pilots of 'B' Flight 41 Squadron. Being religious (for the press)

The Spitfire XII Wing (41 and 91 Squadrons),
Tangmere 1944

Spitfire XII

The author with others 'sailing' in the Lake District

After the wedding – the author and Sylvia

The author celebrating his 70th birthday with his family

CHAPTER XXIV

In January 1945 I went up to Cambridge, leaving Sylvia in York with her parents. We called the baby in her womb Ruth/Michael and planned that the birth should take place at the Purey-Cust nursing home in York. I got digs in Lensfield Road and started my studies in French and German with Donald Beves and a Dr Bolgar, whom I don't remember well. Donald Beves on the other hand was a most memorable character and I continued to have him as my tutor right through my time at King's. He was a great listener and encourager, a lover of drama and of old silver. He shared his enthusiasms and showed what certainly seemed to be a genuine interest in mine. I used to look forward eagerly to my tutorials with him, when I, with two other students of French, would read our essays and listen to his criticisms and each others'. Lively discussion always ensued. I was amazed how quickly I got back into this kind of intellectual exercise after more than four years of the very different life in the RAF.

Another character I got to know – much less easily – was the dean, Archibald Graham-Campbell. He was incredibly silent and shy. I was told I had to call on him, which I was happy enough to do, seeing that he was the man chiefly responsible for the religious life of the college and its famous and beautiful chapel. After knocking on his door and being bidden to enter, I went in to find him standing in front of his fireplace, silent. I introduced myself, saying I was the brother of John Graham, whom he must already know. He said 'Yes', and swayed gently backwards and forwards without further words. I said I'd come up to read modern languages. He said, 'Yes'. Another silence ensued and I couldn't decide which of us was the more embarrassed. I said after some two minutes of this silence, 'I've been in the RAF.'

'Yes', he said, and the gentle swaying continued. By now I was wondering how I was to get away, for it didn't appear that he had anything to say to me. Then I said, 'I'm fairly newly married and my wife is expecting our first baby in March.'

'Good', he said, and then added, 'You are always welcome to come and talk to me.' That I took as a cue for my departure; so I said goodbye and left.

I think I got very little out of the lectures I attended. The real education I got at Cambridge came from late night discussions in the rooms of various undergraduates who had rooms in college and of course from my tutorials with Donald Beves. I wondered if I should do anything athletic but decided against, partly because I didn't want to make any commitments that might keep me away from Sylvia more than necessary after I'd managed to get her to Cambridge; and partly because I still wasn't physically very fit. My back niggled a bit and my piles were getting troublesome.

Regretfully I parted with my car, selling it to my old friend and teacher Hallam McDiarmid. At Cambridge we were well supported with a government grant but running a car was beyond our means and anyway in Cambridge everyone went everywhere by bicycle. We must in fact have been very well off for my first term, when I was still officially in the RAF, enjoying my demobilisation leave, with a special leave allowance and a marriage allowance as well as the grant I got for my university studies.

The 8 March brought me the great news that I was the father of Michael who weighed seven pounds two ounces. and who was, so the midwife said, obviously going to be a bishop. What I noticed as soon as I saw him was that he was just like my father, who of course did happen to be a bishop. I got up to York as fast as I could and spent a few days there before returning to Cambridge, where I set about looking for suitable accommodation for the three of us. I was slightly saddened by the fact that my beloved wife had been virtually unconscious at the actual moment of giving birth. We guessed on reflection later that going private had been a mistake we would not repeat.

Back in Cambridge I had two things to deal with, first finding suitable accommodation for my family, which didn't prove too difficult: I booked us in to an unfurnished flat in Lyndewode Road. It was on the ground floor of a three-story house, the owner of which occupied a bedsitter being the only room on our floor that wasn't to be in our possession.

The second thing was to get something done about my piles. My GP got me into Addenbrookes Hospital, where I underwent surgery that saw me back at work the next day, still pretty uncomfortable but on the mend. The trouble did not get bad again for several years.

I rejoined Sylvia and Michael for the Easter vacation at her sister's home in Cheshunt. Soon after my arrival I got a letter from my future landlady telling me that she had not been able to get her furniture out of the flat we'd booked; so the terms had to be changed. She would now charge us three guineas a week instead of the two guineas we'd agreed on. It didn't seem practicable to start a new search when there was so little time available; so we reluctantly accepted the new conditions, put some bits and pieces of furniture in store and went together to our new first home.

It was a bit of a nightmare. Our landlady required us to keep the kitchen range going. It was coal-fired and heated her water as well as ours while we paid for the coal. She later demanded that we not dry nappies in front of the fire in her/our front room. She had a dog that barked every time anyone came in by the front door; so, since she had eight tenants in all, the dog spent almost half its day barking. Her own kitchenette was situated right outside our kitchen and she was always around when we moved from one of our rooms to the other. The bathroom was upstairs and cost a shilling a bath. The straw that broke the camel's backs was the shock we got when she knocked and entered our bedroom shortly after midnight one night to tell us that the kitchen range was going too hard and we must shut it down or we'd have the water boiling.

Immediately after this we hunted in the local paper for housing ads and in next to no time had agreed to buy a house in Lichfield Road for £2,000. I've no doubt this was a foolish purchase and we could have done better if we'd been prepared to put more time and energy into it. It was only when we came to exchanging contracts that we discovered that the man selling us the house was the tenant not the owner. He was buying it as the sitting tenant for £1,250 at the same time as he was selling it to us with a cool profit of £750. It was about the smallest semi-detached three-bedroomed house possible. Hot water was obtained via a back boiler in the sitting room, which realistically could only be used in winter time and even then, owing to the coal shortage, we often had to burn coke on it, which was very difficult. There was also in the bathroom a geyser that produced hot water so slowly that it took some ten minutes to run a decent bath and, over the kitchen sink, an ascot. In spite of all this we were proud to be home owners and set about making a reasonable garden out of the wasteland behind the house.

Buying the house used all our resources. I never thought for one moment of seeking a mortgage. But we didn't have anything over to buy the furniture we needed. In the end we borrowed from my brother John, who let us have £200, which was sufficient to provide us with the bare necessities. Very generously and on principle he wouldn't accept any interest on the loan, which we only repaid when we'd sold the house some two and a half years later.

It was during my second term at Cambridge that I went to the Careers Office to see if I could forward my intention of becoming a teacher. I told them I wanted to get into the Cambridge Teachers Training College in the autumn of 1948 after getting my degree. 'You're much too early,' they told me, 'come back at the beginning of your last year up.'

I told our landlady what we were doing and she said she supposed I'd want to renege on our contract, which was for three months' rent in advance – already paid. Though I felt I was thoroughly entitled to be let off at least the last month's rent in view of her having previously reneged on our agreement to have the flat unfurnished, I said I didn't mind letting her have the three months' rent though we would only be in occupation for two of them.

So we left amicably and took possession of our first own home, which was a vast improvement on the flat. My main home preoccupation was the garden, in which I made a path of concrete slabs with a few steps in it, which a bit later Michael would love to ride down on his little trike. There was a shed but it had no floor; so I bought some tongue-and-grooved timber and built one. I also sought advice from Granhardy as to what to grow in the way of vegetables and whether it was worth doing anything before the spring. He was very helpful and told me to plant at once spring cabbage which would do all right in undug soil. The rest of the vegetable plot I dug over and by Christmas it was looking good. I also bought and planted six gooseberry bushes. There was a tiny lawn in the front of the house and a small flowerbed in which I planted daffodil bulbs – just twelve of them, being all we could afford.

I decided to do six hours of academic work a day in term time and four hours in the vacations. This left me a good deal of leisure time for work on the house and garden and for time with Sylvia and Michael.

Six hours may not seem very much but I reckon it was probably more than most undergraduates managed. What I did miss out on was late evening talk in other students' rooms. Instead we had a social life with other married undergrads and to a lesser extent with neighbours.

After a year and two terms I sat for my Modern & Medieval Languages Tripos Part 1 in French and German and managed to get a 2:1 in both subjects. For my last year I decided to stick to French only for my Part 2.

This meant studying French philosophy and history, whereas the first part of the tripos had simply been about knowing the language.

At the start of my final year I went back to the Careers Office and told them I wanted now to be enrolled in the Cambridge Teachers Training College. 'Oh dear!' was the response, 'I'm afraid you're much too late. There are no vacancies and there's a waiting list.' I reminded them that they'd told me to come back at precisely this time but I couldn't alter the situation. 'You don't really have to worry', I was then told. 'Lots of people get teaching jobs without going to a training college. If you get a good degree there will be plenty of schools which will have you.' This of course was true but I've always regretted not having had the experience of a college of education. I didn't expect my degree or even my limited experience of teaching at the Manor House to fit me for the sort of job I was likely to get.

Seeing how the land lay I then said I supposed that they'd better put me on their books as someone who wanted a teaching post where I could use my French and German. Very soon after this I was summoned to an interview with a Canon Bonhote, Headmaster of Haileybury & Imperial Service College. The interview went smoothly and at the end of it he said he would be glad to appoint me as French Sixth Form master with effect from September 1948. He also told me that he would have retired by that time but his successor would, he was sure, be glad to have me.

Michael was a great delight to us but I don't think we treated him all that well. I know we used to leave him overlong to cry in his pram at the bottom of the garden because it wasn't yet time for his feed. Much worse, when he was toddling around one day in the spring when he was just two years old, I arrived home from a lecture to find him handing daffodil heads to passers-by and saw that he'd removed the heads of all my dozen superb King Alfred daffs. Unmindful of his generous instincts, conscious merely of my own loss, I spanked him hard.

I made a bit of a mess of the exams at the end of my time at Cambridge, writing far too much about one particular author, much of whose work I'd learnt by heart and dished up, giving the impression – not entirely erroneously – that I knew very little about nineteenth-century French writers other than Stendhal. However they gave me a 2:1 as they'd done for my Tripos Part 1. and I was well satisfied with that. Dear Donald Beves actually said he thought I'd get a first and perhaps stay on at Cambridge to pursue an academic career.

CHAPTER XXV

On arrival at Haileybury I learned that Canon Bonhote was known to everyone as the Boot. His successor, Mr Smith, rather unenterprisingly became the New Boot. He wasn't immediately popular with the teaching staff because he was in the habit of sending out numerous notes rather than talking to us face to face. I thought he was brilliant and very encouraging of me: I found the job much harder than I'd expected.

My main work was very enjoyable: teaching French and subsequently Divinity also to the Sixth Form was almost pure joy but in the lower forms I found it impossible to keep the discipline needed. I learned that if I wanted to get through a session with fifth formers I had to spend a good hour preparing each fifty-minute lesson. The only snag about the sixth was the amount the pupils used to write when I set them essays. I remember on one occasion staying up until 5 a.m. going through their effusions.

We shared a house with the Rogers family. Val was a priest and an English teacher as well as half the chaplaincy team. Mary, his wife, was a scatty charmer, highly intelligent and good company. They had a boy called Bruce who was much the same age as our Michael. The two became fast friends and were joined by a third party who was invisible – to us anyway. His name was Rozzer. His character was wicked. Sometimes he frightened the boys; sometimes he could be a useful person to blame for whatever devilry they'd been up to.

There was one occasion when I was walking home from the school and as I neared our garden I heard the sound of smashing glass. This was Rozzer of course. I yelled 'Stop that!' and the noise ceased. On arriving at the scene of the racket I discovered that almost half of my big tomato cloches were in ruins and glass splinters were widely scattered around the tomatoes which had just lost their shelter. I don't think Rozzer was actually involved in the worst mess Michael got into when he tried to light a dead firework while sitting on our bed. Neither of his parents have a clue as to how he got hold of a box of matches. We were just so lucky that we arrived on the scene in time to prevent a major fire. What we did get was a hole in a sheet, a scorched blanket and a properly frightened little son.

Our daughter Rachel was born at home when we'd been a year at Haileybury. This birth was an altogether happier affair than Michael's had been. This time Sylvia and I both studied natural childbirth as taught by Dr Grantly Dick Read. This time we were determined that mother, with assistance from father, would be in control and would enjoy the great occasion. For me that came to pass one hundred per cent. It was a fantastic joy to see my daughter's head pop out and then the whole of her arrive – just about an hour after the midwife had joined us and taken charge. Up until then I'd been engaged in back-rubbing and generally encouraging. I wouldn't for a moment belittle the travail of any mother but I can say with certainty that this experience was a great one for both of us and I hope not too bad for Rachel. When our doctor turned up Rachel was already dressed and Sylvia tolerably comfortable.

Our bedroom, in which this birth took place, was superb with highly polished parquet floor and a gorgeous great fireplace, where for the odd very special occasion we would have a log fire burning. It had been a billiard room or ballroom in the great old days. Just off it was a partitioned space in what had been the great bow window for the whole room. This made an ideal baby's room.

Outside we shared a glorious garden with a tennis court and an orchard. We played a fair bit of tennis until Sylvia's pregnancy made it less attractive. I made a right hash of the orchard when I tried to grow some potatoes in it. These were completely destroyed by wireworms and leatherjackets. The fruit was mostly pretty good though.

Towards the end of my first term I asked the head if he could give me any advice about my disciplinary problems with fifth formers. He said he'd sit in on one of my classes. Of course while he was in the room everyone behaved angelically. My lesson went exactly as planned but it was by no means a wasted exercise, for talking with me afterwards Mr Smith pointed out a number of things I'd done which might have lead to trouble. He was however very positive and I was grateful and did profit a bit without ever becoming the stern disciplinarian I would like to have been with that particular group of boys.

Virtually all the masters got involved in some sporting activity. It so happened that there was a need for someone to join the art master in teaching sailing. So I took it on and loved it. We did our sailing in twelve-foot national dinghies on the tiny River Lea near Broxbourne. I was, I think, the only lucky member of the sailing group never to get capsized; which was quite a feat considering the amount of tacking we had to do, the extreme flukiness of the wind and the lack of experience of many crewmembers.

We used to go shopping in Hoddesden and soon after our arrival I spotted in the window of an antique dealer a large desk which I thought very attractive and something that would fulfil a real need. It was priced at £100. I went into the shop and asked about the desk's origin and had a good study of it. It had a couple of secret compartments; it was full of curves and covered in marquetry. I said I'd give £50 for it. The dealer laughed and said 'No hope. It's worth every penny of what I'm asking.' After that I used to pop in about once a fortnight. The desk was still sitting in the window. The price was still £100. After about two months I went in and said 'Look, here's my 'phone number. Just ring me when your price comes down to £50.' Some two months after that I got the 'phone call: the desk was mine. I was thrilled and as soon as it had been delivered I filled virtually all of it and my study was tidier as well as greatly enhanced in beauty.

I wasn't far into my second year at Haileybury when I began to think seriously that maybe school-teaching shouldn't be my life-long career. I was beginning to think the unthinkable: that in spite of all my protestations maybe I was meant to be a priest. At least, I thought, I should see somebody and talk about it. I decided to see the bishop, Philip Loyd, and made a date with him. He was encouraging and urged me to go to a selection board with CACTM (the Church's Advisory Council for Training for the Ministry). This was meant to test people's vocation and going there didn't commit me to going forward with plans for ordination. On the other hand I couldn't go forward unless the Board approved of my doing so. I followed this up and in due course found myself in Lichfield, gathered with about a dozen other men seeking ordination and facing three clergymen and one layman who were there to assess our suitability.

I sailed through the process and, as I'd more or less expected, was recommended for training. One man shared with us that this was his fifth attempt to get into the Church's ordained ministry; he'd already tried the Methodists, the Baptists, the Presbyterians and the Congregationalists, but in spite of his certainty that God was calling him nobody seemed to want him! I don't think anyone was surprised that he got the same dusty answer from our selectors.

Having got thus far I became certain in my own mind that I really was meant to be a priest. My next step therefore was to see Canon Cyril Hudson, the Diocesan Director of Ordinands. Later on I was to get to know him well and find him most helpful; but my early experience of him was distinctly unfavourable. To begin with he was rich. I think most of the money had come from his wife who was the sister of either W.D. or H.O. Wills – or both of them. (They were one of the biggest tobacco companies in those days when smoking was still respectable and believed to be harmless.) On top of that he seemed quite incapable of understanding me. He said at first that there was no chance I could go forward to ordination: I hadn't the money to support my wife and children, and nobody was going to give it to me during the two years of training that would be required at a theological college. When I'd told him that I had about £2,000 in savings he said he supposed it might just be possible but I must get every possible grant I could from bodies such as the Catholic Ordination Candidates' Fund. On top of that the diocese would put up £300 per annum towards my college fees; a slight downward adjustment to this would be made if I was successful in getting a fair bit of grant-aid from elsewhere.

In the end, after no little sweat, I managed to secure promises of grants totalling £200 a year. On reporting this to Cyril Hudson by letter I got a reply saying, 'Well done. That means we shall only be giving you £100 from diocesan funds.' I wrote a very angry letter back saying it seemed to me that I was being totally rejected and treated grossly unfairly, indeed downright dishonestly. To which he replied that he'd warned me that I wasn't able with my family commitments to afford the training. Perhaps all his discouragement was a ploy to get me vigorously tested. Anyway, I said I'd go forward and find the money needed somehow.

Now that the die was cast I went to share with the New Boot what I'd been up to. He wasn't surprised and was very kind, even saying that in his opinion I would in fact have become a very good teacher if I'd chosen to stay on. Many of my friends and relations had been suggesting for years that I ought to 'go into the Church' and now they were pleased that I was doing the obviously right thing.

One more hurdle had to be jumped and that was a medical test. All through my time at Haileybury I'd had back trouble and had paid periodic visits to a physiotherapist. The pain was never crippling and the situation had improved steadily; so I wasn't expecting any difficulty when I reported to a Harley Street physician, appointed by the Church to test my fitness for ordination. Indeed it did all go well but on running his hand down my spine he suddenly asked, 'When did you get this dislocation?' Of course I said I didn't know anything about any dislocation. Then we went through my life story or at least the last few years, which led him to the conclusion that it happened when I baled out of my Spitfire. He said I could have an operation to put it right but he wouldn't recommend it, saying that my back had by now pretty well adjusted to the situation and I'd best leave it alone. He did add that he thought it was quite wrong of the RAF to have discharged me as A1 but that there was nothing now from the health point of view to stop me entering the ordained ministry.

CHAPTER XXVI

The big question now was which theological college I should try to get into. I wanted somewhere that was in the Catholic wing of the Church but couldn't consider either Cuddesdon, which I knew too well, or Cheshunt, about which most of the things I heard were unfavourable – at least to married men. In the end I plumped for my brother John's college which was Ely. He spoke well of it. I didn't really give half enough thought to what it would mean for Sylvia. She had accepted my vocation with great understanding and never held it against me in spite of my earlier assurances that I'd never ever do what her father had done to her mother by changing from being a schoolmaster to being a clergyman.

I went to see Canon Henry Balmforth, the Principal of Ely, and asked him to accept me. He told me that there was one big snag; wives and girlfriends were not allowed to live within ten miles of the college. I suppose that should have put me off for good, but it didn't. So I spent a lot of time house-hunting and looking for possible part-time jobs to go with a new home.

Eventually we spotted an advertisement. The squire of Wilburton, a village just six miles from Ely, wanted a housekeeper to look after his home and his mother and to live in a separate flat. This looked promising and we went to be interviewed. We were told we would hear from him soon; but the next event was that he summoned us to see him in his chambers, he being a London solicitor. On arrival he told us immediately that he couldn't offer Sylvia the housekeeping job. Our hearts sank. Was Sylvia, we wondered, too young or were the children the problem? But no; Mr Pell thought she was too much of a lady for the job he had in mind. 'I wonder though,' he went on, 'whether you'd be interested in quite another proposition. I own a rather charming Tudor cottage which used to be the Post Office and before that the bakery. It has half an acre of garden and orchard, completely overgrown with weeds and rubbish. I thought perhaps you might like to restore the garden to decent order, do a bit of work on some of my farmland and occupy the cottage rent-free. I would of course pay you for whatever time you could spend on my land and you could use my rotavator to help you get your garden straight.

This offer seemed almost too good to be true so we accepted it there and then. The principal waived the ten mile rule, about which we'd conveniently forgotten. The cottage was indeed charming. It had a few little snags, such as a concrete floor in the kitchen and one of the three bedrooms being also a passage way and a nasty modern grate having been installed in the sitting room where once there had been a massive open fireplace. It was however a much better property than anything else we'd seen; and to have it rent-free was a very big bonus given our parlous financial situation.

Our landlord was really doing this as a way of doing his bit for the Church. We were truly thankful that we'd come across such a generous benefactor. Sylvia Fletcher-Moulton, that great friend of my aunt Christian also gave us notable financial help. In the end we were able to prove Cyril Hudson wrong but I could now see that he'd had a point when he'd said I couldn't afford to get ordained.

Term time was tough on Sylvia and the children, for though I came out four times a week on my motor bike she found it a lonely life, good though she always was at making friends. I worked very hard in the garden whenever I was at home and it became fruitful in quick time. Seeing it had been covered in the biggest nettles I've ever seen before or since, I knew I had wonderfully rich soil. The nettles when composted simply added more richness. I was able to dig a trench three spits deep and some forty feet long in one day in preparation for growing sweet peas, which in due time were to produce quite a nice income for us. In the vacations I put in quite a lot of work for Mr Pell, who knew nothing at all about growing things but paid me half a crown an hour for various jobs, some OK and some foolish, like the planting of two thousand lettuces in one of his fields without making any plans for harvesting or selling them.

In order to mitigate Sylvia's loneliness I had the bright idea of getting her a puppy. I found a very sweet mongrel whose mother was a spaniel. I guess his father must have been a cross between a great dane and a giant poodle, for he swiftly grew to a gigantic size and needed to be walked for some ten miles a day to subdue his appetite for exercise. Of course Sylvia couldn't possibly have done what was required. As a result Tigger, as we called him because he was so bouncy, used to try to eat the furniture, pull clothes off the washing line and knock over our little Rachel. In the end he had to go and we found a farmer who was glad to take him off our hands.

My life was full. Apart from the many jobs to be done at Wilburton I had my theological studies and social activities in the college. I joined two of the societies there, one was a theological group, where each member in turn read a learned paper and was then subjected to questions and criticisms. We used to stick up on the college notice board the subject and the speaker for the next meeting. When my turn came I delivered a paper on the mystical theology of Dionysius the Areopagite. To my amazement the principal came and joined us for my paper and professed himself most impressed by it.

We had the same sort of programme in the other society which was called the Broughal Biographical Club or BBC. In this group I produced two biographies: Bishop Tommy Strong, whom I had known as a child, and Augustus Carp, the fictitious autobiographer of his book *A Really Good Man*. I had great fun with both characters, neither of whom was known by anyone else in the club.

I played cricket rather well by village and college cricket standards and was made captain of the college side though we acquired a much better player than myself soon after my appointment. This was Graham Dowell, a most remarkable bearded blonde who had the Midas touch. He was a brilliant football, tennis and cricket player, who was likely to hit at least three sixes every time he batted, to serve three aces in every tennis service game and to score at least two goals if he was playing in a football match. He also had a Cambridge double first and used to cause acute embarrassment to Robert Daubeny, the Vice-Principal, who lectured us on Biblical Theology and who was frequently non-plussed by Graham's penetrating questions.

By the summer of 1951 our Wilburton garden was so well developed that I could make a bit of money selling vegetables and sweet peas. I used to provide a hotel in Ely with almost all the flowers they wanted and I kept the bishop in vegetables. He asked me always to check whether he was at home and available when I delivered his consignment. When he was at home he often had a quick chat with me, seeming to like having a safe listening ear into which he could pour out some of his troubles with misbehaving clerics who seemed to abound in his diocese. This certainly gave me a useful insight into an aspect of the Church's life of which I was quite ignorant. Up to this time I suppose I'd held the common view that clergymen took services and helped other people in various ways without ever needing any help themselves. I had been virtually unaware that there were such people as erring clergy, depressed clergy, clergy with marriage problems – in fact clergy who were no better or healthier than their parishioners.

Henry Balmforth had suggested that I prepare for Ely before I joined the College by reading Baron von Hugel's *The Mystical Element of Religion*, or at least the first three chapters of it. In fact I became fascinated by the book and had read it from cover to cover before I began my formal training. Of course there were other subjects that had to be studied, but I kept an accurate record of my reading while at Ely and in the end read more books on mystical and ascetical theology than on all other subjects put together.

My reading led me to think of writing a book myself on the subject of marriage and prayer. I never got anywhere near completing this project and decided that since I wasn't keen on thorough research, a scholarly work was beyond me. I did however rough out a scheme of the book and used it some years later when I wrote a paper for a theological society which used to meet in Oxford. The paper was published by the Church's Board for Social Responsibility in its journal, which used then to sport the ghastly title *Moral Welfare*. What I aimed to share as widely as possible was my passionate belief that we could learn much about our relationship with God from our experience of marriage and much about how to live better married lives from our experience of God. The strange thing was that while I was prone to thinking much on these things I was failing pretty miserably as a husband but having a whale of a time in my relationship with God. I was enjoying over again the kind of ecstatic experience that was mine for some three years while I was a boy at Teddy's. I wasn't really aware how hard it was for Sylvia, stuck out in the country in a village where many of the inhabitants had never travelled further than the six miles to Ely.

In December 1951 my father was diagnosed as having cancer and needing urgent major surgery. Only three years earlier he'd had a bad accident when he was thrown off a London bus as he was getting on board. He was badly smashed up and off work for several months. When he did come back he was very lame and told he would henceforth always have to walk with a stick. Knowing that his chances of survival were only about even I wrote him a long letter telling him about my own abundantly joyful mystical experience and thanking him extensively for all the many blessings that had come to me through him. I got a lovely letter back, the one big surprise in it for me was that he shared among many other things the fact that he had never *felt* the reality of God. I thought and still think how unfair this was. Here was a man who spent more time in prayer than anyone else I knew, plodding faithfully on, feeling nothing; whereas I, giving far less, was receiving far more.

In the end he made a complete recovery and I noticed two great goods that came out of this: his lameness had ended and his relationship with me had reached a new and most satisfying closeness. Obviously there were many other good things, including the further eight years he had before retirement from his diocese.

CHAPTER XXVII

From the start of my second year at Ely I was on the lookout for suitable jobs after ordination. It was clear that one's first curacy was of vital importance because training in the practical side of priestly ministry only really began in the parish. I was determined that my first vicar should be something of a superman who would know all the answers and be quite unlike the men who so troubled the Bishop of Ely.

A little while later I received an invitation to visit the Dean of St Albans with a view to my possibly being offered a job on his staff. Cuthbert Thicknesse was a formidable priest in every way. Like most of the dignitaries of the St Albans Diocese he had a severe limp, caused by a First World War wound to his knee. (Of the other dignitaries the Bishop of Bedford had Parkinson's and Canon Douglas Feaver, the Sub-Dean, had flat feet, while the archdeacon and Canon Hudson walked pretty well normally.) Dean Thicknesse gave me to understand that I would probably fit the bill; this would involve me in having pastoral care of half the parish under the overall oversight of the sub-dean; and acting as Precentor in the Cathedral on those occasion when the real precentor was away. The Precentor was Norman Hill who looked after the other half of the parish. The dean at the end of my interview told me that because he had two daughters, one son-in-law and eight grandchildren staying in the deanery I'd have to spend the night with the Feavers next door. He also said I'd better get over there soon after supper as the Feavers liked to get to bed early and the sub-dean would certainly want to get to know me and pronounce on my suitability or otherwise.

As soon as I'd arrived at the Old Rectory, Douglas Feaver sat me down in his study, asked after my family and then plunged straight into research as to my knowledge of matters theological. The only part of this conversation I recall clearly went something like this:

D.F.:   'What interesting books have you been reading lately?'

P.G.:   'The one I've just finished is *The Mystery of Love and Marriage* by Dr Sherwin Bailey. I've also recently read a ridiculous review of it in the *Church Times*. The anonymous reviewer used his space simply to pick out odd-sounding phrases, quoted out of context and made fun of, while telling us nothing at all about the actual theme of the book.'

D.F.:   'I wrote it.'

At that time I'd no idea that the *Church Times* was more or less run by the senior staff of St Albans Abbey. The editor was Rosamund Essex, who was a key member of the abbey congregation; the dean spent the whole of his day off nearly every week working for the paper; and the sub-dean was one of its principal reviewers. None of these were the least bit petty people and I couldn't have had a better start in my relationship with Douglas Feaver, who was to be my mentor as much as the dean.

I spent a whole Sunday in St Albans. After Cathedral Evensong I went for a quiet prayer time into the choir. Kneeling in that area was Bishop Philip Loyd, who had delivered the sermon. To my astonishment a loud voice boomed out from the vestry, the other side of a screen from where the bishop and I were kneeling. It was a voice I knew: it belonged to Canon Cyril Hudson. 'Not much of a preacher, our bishop, is he?' went the voice. A short silence ensued, after which the dean could be only just heard saying: 'If the bishop were to stand in that pulpit for five minutes simply saying "Rhubarb, rhubarb, Mrs Atkinson" we'd all go home the better for it. You've only to look at the man. He's a Saint.'

One important hurdle was still to be jumped: Sylvia had to come and look at the house and the job; only then could I accept. She came. She looked at the house, which was splendid and we came to lunch at the deanery. At the dining table there were the dean and his wife Rhoda, plus a very aged and very deaf aunt of the dean's. This was quite the worst meal I've ever had, not excluding those I'd had in Germany. The first course was macaroni cheese. Cooked cheese is a dish that I loathe. By eating very slowly and drinking lots of water I managed more or less to get through it. The next course was rhubarb tart. When we'd all been served, the aged aunt, picking at it with a hopeless look on her face asked, 'What is this, Cuthbert?' To which his Very Reverence replied, 'It's horrible, raw, uncooked rhubarb, Auntie.' Rhoda Thicknesse smiled sweetly – as was her wont at all times – and we did our best to eat some of it.

All parties were satisfied and so I became Assistant Curate Designate of the Cathedral and Abbey Church of St Alban with a stipend of £350 a year and a pleasant three-bedroomed house near the bottom of Abbey Mill Lane. The house was still then occupied by my predecessor, Stephen Adams, who passed over to me in due time a most thorough block of files, card indexing everyone in our part of the parish. He'd visited every household and some of them many times, each visit being recorded with comments which were illuminating, sometimes helpful and always interesting.

At this stage I was expecting to take up my post after ordination at Michaelmas, the end of September. I'd already completed the General Ordination Examination to the satisfaction of the examiners; so I was looking forward to a fairly easy last term at Ely with the opportunity to get started on my book. At Wilburton my second summer's crops were in good form. In particular, following success with my sweet peas the previous year, I'd got some hundred plants growing as single cordons up eight-foot bamboo canes, which should in theory produce at least fifty show-sized blooms every day from May to September.

Out of the blue came a letter from Dean Thicknesse, in which he said he much regretted that it would be necessary for me to get ordained at the Trinity Ordination and so join his staff four months earlier than we'd planned. This was because Stephen Adams had left earlier than expected, so that the house in Abbey Mill Lane was now vacant and couldn't be left that way. Someone would have to occupy it; if it were not to be us it would be somebody else, which would leave us without accommodation. The choice was stark: 'Come now or lose your house.'

There was no question about it: we had to go. From several points of view this was a blessing. Sylvia would cease to have to live without me for half the time. I would at last be earning some money, meagre though the stipend was. Finally it was good to get going in my new calling as soon as was possible. Against that there were two sadnesses: first, I'd lost the chance of writing my book and having a fairly leisurely final term; second, my summer plans for market gardening had to be abandoned. This involved selling my lovely sweet pea plants for two pence each, which I was lucky to get, and parting with quite a lot of equipment for next to nothing.

Early in May we moved to Abbey Mill Lane. We all travelled in the pantechnicon which held my motor bike as well as all our furniture, some of which was well arranged at the back to provide us with comfortable seating and a view out. We settled in comfortably and fixed Michael up at St Michael's Church School, which was some ten minutes' walk from the house – a walk that took one past the lovely Verulam Lake and the River Ver.

My last few days before ordination were spent in retreat and then on 8 June 1952 I was ordained deacon in the abbey by our new bishop, Michael Gresford-Jones. He lived in Abbey Gate House where I'd been interviewed by his predecessor. This was only some fifty yards up the road from us, so that I often met the bishop, occasionally finding him on horseback. Twice on such occasions he stopped and asked me if I could do with a bit of financial help. Both times I said 'yes'. Both times he handed me a fiver from his discretionary fund. His wife, Lucy was also most kind to us.

CHAPTER XVIII

I doubt if at any other time of my life I learned so much in such a short time. There was something new to pick up just about every day of my year as a deacon. On my first Sunday after ordination I was required to assist with the chalice at three Communion services. The 9.30 a.m. Family Eucharist was the big one. We had about four hundred communicants served by four clergy. The chalice I had to administer was vast but was still necessarily almost full to the brim when I began my administration. Long before I'd finished I thought I'd never manage to get through without dropping it. Of course I survived without mishap and this task got easier as the weeks went by.

I was allowed to have a whole month before I was required to deliver my first sermon. All through my time as a deacon I had to produce my sermons in full, typewritten and double spaced to allow for the dean's corrections in red pencil. These had to be submitted to him three days before they were due to be delivered and were handed back to me, sometimes with additional verbal comments, at the regular Friday morning staff meeting.

Staff meetings were fascinating. For some of the time we had a laywoman with us – Doris Roy. She was a wonderful person who helped me no end with good advice always delivered in a humble way. She also came round with me whenever I took Communion to the housebound. She used to go on ahead and get everything ready at each house we visited, leaving almost immediately after I'd finished my sacramental ministrations, so that she could do the same job at the next house while I could have a shot at giving a wee bit of extra pastoral care to the householder.

The dean was very clearly boss, though Douglas Feaver often argued furiously with him on theological issues. The dean listened but always ended by asserting his authority. He was fond of referring to 'my cathedral'. Once indeed he'd red-pencilled a bit of one of my sermons where I'd referred to the stinking feet which Christ washed. 'I won't have the word "stinking" used in my cathedral', he told me.

Either Norman Hill or I would sing the offices of Morning and Evening Prayer each weekday with the choir and a few old people. On Wednesdays and Fridays there was no choir but we were still obliged to sing the service. One day there was no congregation other than the verger and the two of us. Norman said, 'We'll *say* the office.' He started away and I responded; barely three lines into it a voice came bellowing but tunefully from the vestry with the next response. Of course we then had to complete our work singing instead of sinning as we'd begun to do according to the dean, who was very angry. 'In my cathedral the office is *sung* every day', he insisted.

I'd not been long in the parish when the Queen came to Evensong one Sunday after being present at the consecration of one of the seven new churches in the diocese. I occupied a clergy stall just a yard away from the front pew in the nave, which was occupied by Her Majesty, the Duke of Edinburgh and the Lord High this and the Lady that. As a result of this proximity my mind was less than a hundred per cent on my job. In fact the only special thing I had to do was to leave my stall when the last hymn had started and precede the dean to the sanctuary, where I would bow him in and then pick up the vast alms dish and return to the centre ready to receive the numerous bags of money that would be brought up by the sidesmen.

I forgot all about it. When the third verse had begun and I was still stationary a stentorian voice roared, 'Peter, you fool, wake up!' Every eye in the royal pew turned to see who this fool was. I felt the colour rising throughout my body and a scarlet-faced junior curate moved hastily from stall to centre aisle and then, with what dignity I could manage, got to the place where I stood aside to bow the dean into the sanctuary. A great hand came out and clasped mine; above that hand was a face as red as my own. 'Can you ever forgive me?' said the dean. Of course I did. I'd learned another valuable lesson from him: it's OK to express anger and if you hurt someone apologise at once.

Shortly after this I was asked to look after Geoffrey Fisher, Archbishop of Canterbury who was to preach in the abbey. I was required to lead a great procession from Abbey Gate House, our bishop's residence, ending up in the nave sanctuary where I would sit beside the archbishop and see that he was happy. The route was a matter of guesswork, which bothered me a bit but nobody objected to the route I selected. As soon as we were settled in and the service was under way the archbishop asked me, 'Is there a glass of water in the pulpit?' I said I didn't know. 'Well then, will you kindly find out!', he said, 'and if there isn't, get one there.'

Two years later Geoffrey Fisher visited us again and to my astonishment immediately on entering the clergy vestry walked up to me and said, 'Hello, Peter; good to see you again. Tell me how your father's getting on.' I thought that was pretty good going even for a well-briefed dignitary. There were at least ten other clergy present and he was evidently aware that my father might still be adjusting to life with a sheep's oesophagus.

Cuthbert Thicknesse was a great teacher. At first I accompanied him on every conceivable kind of pastoral work so that I could observe his methods and discuss them afterwards. He could be frightening but in his pastoral ministrations he was gentleness personified. Dougie Feaver was perhaps even more frightening at times than the dean; but he had a heart of gold, was very kind to me when I was ill; and he was a magnificent preacher.

My tutor, whose task it was to see that I continued to study the job and the theology behind it, was Canon Cyril Hudson, with whom I'd had such a difficult start. In the end we got on famously though I always felt he was a little out of touch with the real world. He told me for instance that he never spent less than fourteen hours in preparing a sermon. I dare say I did take that long over my first two or three but later I would have to preach three times a Sunday without repeating myself; so two hours was a more appropriate time than fourteen to spend on that job.

Although I didn't have too much preaching to do in the abbey, there was a mission church where I occasionally took Evensong and preached and two Church schools where I had to do a bit of teaching. Then towards the end of my first Lent the dean said to me one day: 'Holy Week will be upon us soon and you will give the devotional addresses to the sisters at Diocesan House.' The sisters were members of the Community of St Mary the Virgin and led by Sister Rachel, who was a formidable character and a first cousin of the bishop. 'I can't do it', I said. 'Of course you can', said the dean. 'Nuns are holy people who will get something out of what any fool tells them.' End of objection. And he was right.

Now the birth of our third child was imminent. This time it was decreed that Sylvia must be in hospital for the birth. We'd had more than a spot of bother through rhesus blood incompatibility between mother and child when Rachel was born. On Easter Day Sylvia was at the Family Eucharist with Michael and Rachel. I had to stay on for Mattins and a late Communion. When I got home the family was at the dinner table. Sylvia said quite casually that she'd been in labour for some three hours. She sometimes pretends that she's never fully forgiven me for depriving her of her dinner that day; for I rushed to the telephone and she was whisked into hospital, where some three hours later I was able to see her and our newborn son Anthony. Cuthbert Thicknesse used to hold Sylvia up as a role model for Christian mothers. 'She came to the Eucharist on Easter morning. She went off and had her baby and was back in church for Evensong', he used to tell people with more mirth than truth.

On Whitsunday, 24 May 1953 I was ordained Priest. This meant that in addition to all the duties of the curacy which I'd already been performing I was now to preside at the Eucharist and could in emergency hear confessions and grant absolution. I had to get the bishop's permission to act as a confessor, the dean having already prescribed some supposedly helpful literature on the subject. It was in fact desperately out of date and I remember being rather stumped by one of my earliest penitents showing me that he had completely different views about what was and was not sinful in the realm of sex. Looking back I think he was much more in the right than I'd been.

One thing I soon learned when this ministry increased was that I needed to do a lot more study of psychology. I'd wanted to do this back at Cambridge but had been put off when I found out that it seemed to be all about the behaviour of rats on treadmills and such stuff, which I stupidly considered totally irrelevant to the study of the human mind and emotions, which was what I was interested in.

One of my most absorbing pastoral encounters was with a man who was deemed to be suffering from shell shock dating back to the First World War. He was obsessional and agoraphobic. He couldn't leave his house because he felt he had to go back and wash his hands if he got more than a yard or two from his door. His poor hands were a sorry sight, almost raw with the scrubbing he gave them. I got to know him well and eventually managed to coax him as far as my house, which was a good half mile from his. Just as I was beginning to think he was a whole person and when the washing had almost got back to normal, he developed cancer of the stomach and became the first person I saw through the process of dying, which I did with the help and example of the dean. It was, and nearly always since then has been, a moving and grace-filled experience. It is around a death that the priest knows he is wanted and it is then above all other times that I and countless others can rejoice in our Christian commitment and share with others our assurance of eternal life with God. One of the pastoral lessons that I learned from Dougie Feaver was, to use his own words, to 'give 'em a smack in the eye while the tears are wet.' Though crudely expressed I grasped what he meant and based much of my evangelistic strategy on that principle. A kindlier way of putting it would perhaps be: 'Show your people you love them and can listen to their grief. That will be better than all the preaching you might hand out.'

CHAPTER XXIX

From the time of my priesting to the present day I've always been aware of a tension between my scientific side, which embraced pastoral psychology and medicine, on the one hand, and on the other my belief in the supernatural. I was never a fundamentalist or biblical literalist but it seems to me quite impossible to understand the Christian Gospel without accepting some element of the supernatural. Many things that were once believed to be miraculous could indeed be explained naturally. I knew that there remained and always would remain happenings that could not be explained by any purely natural science. As my ministry developed I found my emphasis veering more from the supernatural to the natural; a fact that still bothers me. In the early years of my ministry I used frequently to lay hands on the sick with prayer for their recovery and expect them to recover. This indeed happened in amazing ways. Later, when I'd done a great deal of study in the realm of counselling and psychotherapy I found that I moved away from this stance, continued to help people to health but no longer expected or found instant 'success'. I became highly suspicious of quick cures where there was clearly a psychological malfunction.

The most miraculous-looking of the healings in which I got involved was undoubtedly that of a woman in hospital, paralysed from the waist down and unable to feel anything in her legs. Her problem was mystifying the medical staff, but she was someone I already knew and her 'cure' consisted on one not very long thrash about her inability to move psychologically, followed by my ordering her to get up and walk. She did this and found all her feeling returned. Two other healings I shared in the same hospital had less obvious explanations. The first was a woman, who, I was assured by the Ward Sister, was about to die owing to inoperable cancer, upon whom I laid hands with a prayer for her healing, which duly followed, so that she made a complete recovery. The other, just a week or so later, was a parishoner who died the day after I'd ministered to her. She died in peace instead of the torment she had been suffering before. A sceptic could easily say that there was nothing supernatural about any of these events.

The reality of the miraculous was however impossible to deny when one day soon after my ordination I was presiding at a weekday Eucharist in the abbey and accidentally knocked over the chalice of consecrated wine just after I'd finished administering the Sacrament. A great red stain spread across the fair linen cloth on the altar. The moment was as embarrassing as any I'd had. The dean was assisting me and I was as bothered about how he'd take it as about what God would think. When we got to the vestry he summoned the head verger and told him to collect the cloth off the altar and bring it to him. A couple of minutes later the verger was back holding up in front of us a pure white cloth without wrinkle or stain. Why this should have happened I do not know and can't imagine. The dean's only remark was 'Thank you. You can put the cloth back again. We need never be surprised at what the Lord does.'

Probably because of my own very happy mystical life and my special interest in spirituality, I found myself being used by several people as a spiritual director even while I was still only the junior curate. Amazingly I was even asked to conduct a retreat, which took a lot of preparation but seemed to go well. Preaching in the abbey was a bit of an ordeal because there were no microphones in those days and the often vast congregation could only hear the sermon if it was delivered at near full volume and directed straight at the third pillar on the south side of the nave. When I preached for the first time from that pulpit I was horrified to find there were three bishops in the congregation. I don't think I ever got to find it easy to climb the seven steps to that pulpit and start a sermon.

During my third and last year in St Albans I received several offers of livings, all but one of which I dismissed out of hand, being sure that it was too soon to be striking out on my own. One however made me think seriously. This came about through a visit from a John Falwasser who was an old boy of St Edward's and churchwarden of the Parish of Eaton Bray in Bedfordshire. The living was in the gift of the Diocesan Board of Patronage but he believed in taking active steps to ensure that the Board nominated someone the parish would find acceptable. I found John very good company and a keen churchman so thought it worth at least having a look at the parish, which we did.

When the Board of Patronage met and I was summoned to appear before it I found that there were just two other candidates, neither of whom struck me as serious competitors. The bishop was in the Chair and he read out to me the wishes of the parish as expressed in a letter from the PCC. I was amazed to hear that they hoped the new vicar would be a competent organist like the departing one. In other respects I seemed to fill the bill pretty well, though the bishop said: 'As so often we find what the Church Council wants is the Archangel Gabriel – only married.'

This all happened early in 1955 but I was neither free nor anxious to leave the abbey in a hurry. However I was appointed and thus became Vicar Designate of Eaton Bray and the date of my induction was to be 2 July. We then had to prepare to move from our little three-bedroomed house into a vast vicarage with nine bedrooms, four reception rooms, a big hall, two staircases, two kitchens, a scullery, numerous outbuildings and two and a half acres of garden.

Meanwhile life got rather busier for me. I hoped I might emulate Stephen Adams, my predecessor, by visiting every household in my patch at least once. I knew I could never do the same number of visits he had done but at least I had his wonderful card index which told me so much about the people I was to care for that I could visit with some sort of prioritising. One I left for a long time but eventually fitted in had a card that went something like this:

> Miss B. Robertson 809 Holywell Hill.
> Middle-aged to elderly. Difficult.
> She told me her friends called her 'B'
> But is that Bee or Bea?
> My personal choice is for plain B!

One day I did a terrible thing while out visiting with a few of these cards in my pocket and also some letters I had to post. No sooner had I dropped the letters into the pillar box than I discovered I'd dropped one of the cards in too. The box was due to be emptied at a time when I'd have to be in the abbey; so I rushed home and rang up the sorting office. They told me that they'd look out for the card and abstract it if they spotted it. When I rang again to find out what luck they'd had, I was told, 'Sorry mate. It must have gone out with the post.' As soon as I could I went to the house. I'd forgotten the contents of the card except for the address and just hoped it wasn't as awful as Miss Robertson's. Luckily for me the householder, who was a widow living on her own, had a nice sense of humour and laughed in a friendly enough way when I explained what had happened. 'I can't really complain', she said. 'I suppose I *am* middle-aged and I don't go to church. Come in, sit down and feel forgiven.'

One day near the end of our time at St Albans I was working in the garden, dressed in my very old RAF battledress when a message was brought to me from the deanery. 'The dean has had a second heart attack and is very ill. Come at once.' He had been ill for a short time but had been thought to be getting on well. I wasn't at all sure how to proceed but dashed up to the abbey and collected the Reserved Sacrament and the Holy Oil and thus provided went straight to the deanery. The front door was opened by Rhoda Thicknesse, who looked at me and said: 'You can't see the dean looking like that!' I told her I didn't know how urgent it was and she told me it was very urgent. 'I think he's dying,' she said, 'and he thinks so too. Come in and I'll dress you up in some of his gear.' So, wearing a dog-collar five sizes too big and a cassock with a waist at least a foot bigger than my own, covered by a decanal surplice and stole, I entered the great man's room.

There I found a little bedside table beautifully prepared for me with a cloth and lighted candles. The dean was obviously in pain and very tired but still quite capable of talking. 'Hear my confession first please', he said. This I did; it didn't take long. 'Now give me counsel and absolution.'

'I don't think you need much counsel at this point', I said.

'Nonsense. I want counsel and I mean to go on teaching you while I've breath in my body.' I was then able to get through all the rest of what he required, giving him communion, anointing and prayers of commendation of the dying. He hovered between death and life for several days and then began to recover.

Cuthbert Thicknesse, though quite unfit now to exercise his office, was still Dean of St Albans when we moved at the end of June to Eaton Bray. In fact he obstinately refused to retire in spite of all that bishop and sub-dean could do to persuade him. Eventually he did agree to go and exercised a valuable ministry in a small country parish for several more years.

CHAPTER XXX

We were settling in at Eaton Bray Vicarage. There were two wealthy and well-disposed families in the village, both dominated by their women. Our next door neighbours at Poplar Farm were the daughters of Mr Wallace, who had built the great nurseries which had employed half the population. They were Mrs Gray and Mrs Oates. They were very kind to us and immediately on our arrival presented us with a cheque for £75 with which to buy a drawing room carpet. Not long after that Mrs Taylor, a widow as was Mrs Gray, gave me an industrial vacuum cleaner worth even more than the carpet. She told me that I would be able to use her gift on the church and also hire it out to firms who needed their factories cleaned.

On my first Sunday at work I took the traditional three services. After the last of them John Falwasser said to me: 'That was OK but you really don't have to shout like that; you're not in the cathedral now.' With this in mind I lowered my voice the following Sunday only to be confronted after Mattins by an irate Bert Bunker, who was the other churchwarden and a most loveable and outspoken retired miller. 'Last week,' he told me, with the considerable volume of the hard of hearing, 'I thought we'd got a proper vicar. Now we're back to the old mumbling that half of us can't hear.' On the whole I thought this complaint more worthy of notice than the previous one but a compromise was what I aimed at.

Not everyone was best pleased when I took a fortnight's holiday almost at once. We weren't aware at the time but Sylvia had conceived our fourth child before we left St Albans. Now we travelled by train to Dundee (all paid for by my parents) and spent the holiday in their palatial house, Forbescourt in Broughty Ferry. It was not a good time for Sylvia who began by far the worst lot of morning sickness she'd experienced. This was not confined to mornings but just went on and on, so that in the end my mother felt compelled to send for the doctor, who was reassuring but could do little to help.

It was at Forbescourt that the 'pingway' was born. One wet day, ostensibly to amuse the older children, I constructed in one of the unused rooms a kind of railway system made of strings stretched taut some three-quarters of an inch apart between various heavy bits of furniture. The 'trains' that ran along these 'lines' were ping-pong balls. Later, when fine weather came along, I stretched wires between trees in the garden on the same principle, and tried using billiard balls on them. This was hopeless; but on changing the 'trains' to golf balls I met with instant success. With wires in place of strings it was possible to create long stretches of 'rail', kept correctly spaced with 'sleepers' formed by short bits of wire twisted into shape and attached to the 'line' every eighteen inches or so. It was possible to buy second-hand golf balls very cheaply in that area; so I stocked up.

Some years after this Forbescourt was found to be riddled with dry rot; as a result the house was sold and a new and much more suitable one was bought on the other side of the road. This house had a lovely garden sloping down to the main East Coast railway line with a fine view of the Tay estuary beyond it. In the lower part of this garden, with the help of my brother Martin and my sons, I constructed a truly massive pingway with a swing bridge, signalling system, remotely controlled points and a total track length of about a quarter of a mile. We were to spend many of our summer holidays here and the pingway provided endless entertainment for the boys but I fear that it wasn't quite so much fun for Rachel and a positive pain for Sylvia.

Back from holiday there was much to do. Having played no cricket while in St Albans I thought it was high time to have another go. I went along to the nets and demonstrated that I could bowl fairly effectively against the local batsmen. As usual my batting wasn't up to much. I was picked for the first match for which I was available but to my chagrin was not asked to bowl until the game was virtually over. The custom at Eaton Bray, as in many other village cricket teams, was that just two stock bowlers should do all the work. I got in just one over, in which two runs were scored off a dropped catch in the slips and two wickets were taken, both clean bowled by yorkers.

I had arranged to take the service of Evening Prayer at 6.30 p.m. every day except my day off. To my amazement this became a well-attended do. Up to a dozen youngsters came almost every day and I used to explain what it was all about, a little bit each day. Because I'd made this commitment I was unable to play in away cricket matches. I was therefore dropped from the side altogether. On reflection I think this was quite reasonable and I was very stupid not to see that I could perfectly well have had Saturday Evening Prayer at 8 p.m. and made myself free to travel.

One of the things I knew I must do was to check on the condition of the fabric of the church. I therefore asked the Church architect to come as soon as possible and do an inspection and let me have his report. This he did and delivered in December the statement that everything was in order bar a very few minor items which perhaps ought to be seen to in the next few years. On the first Sunday after Easter in the following year I spotted a few little beetles on the church floor. That was in the morning. At afternoon Sunday School I asked all the children to have a beetle hunt and bring me the results. Out of this I got fifty-seven beetles which I put in a box and took next day to another architect, whom I'd met by chance. He told me I'd got death watch beetle in a big way. This was their breeding season when they left the woodwork only to return later in much greater numbers.

I asked him to come and do a thorough inspection of the church. His report stated that the infestation we had must date back many years. We got scaffolding up very quickly and I was asked to push my hand into the main beam at the apex of the chancel roof. When I did this it felt like soft butter, and my fingers went right up through eight inches of timber to be stopped finally by the lead on the top.

I dismissed the official Church architect at once. His excuse was that I hadn't supplied him with ladders, which was true but not much of an explanation for the years of neglect.

So I had to face one of the things I'd dreaded – having to spend lots of time raising money. The architect's estimate was £4,500, which turned out to be very accurate. We had to replace all the timber of the chancel roof and some elsewhere. I soon forgot my qualms and threw myself into the money-raising business with gusto. Two fairly local firms gave us a great start by supplying us with cardboard appeal boxes and the labels to stick on them at no charge. These we distributed to every household in the parish; of whom less than half a dozen refused them.

Once I sat all day outside the church to receive gifts. This was financially rewarding but it also gave many people the chance to have a talk with me so that many relationships were started. Those appeal boxes were collected once a quarter by volunteers from the church, which also turned out to be useful meeting points in a place where there was very little social life.

My first funeral brought me an unexpected embarrassment. The local undertaker was in charge. He was Syd Sharrett, one of two brothers both getting on in years who were fine builders but in other respects somewhat unconventional. Syd was very hard of hearing. When the mourners were all lined up at the churchyard gate he came up to me and shouted: 'How much do I owe you for this lot then, vicar?'

'I'll talk to you later', I replied.

'Did you say eight pund?' came the next shout.

'No; and please leave it for now', I pleaded.

'So you don't want anything, is that it?'

'Do let's just get on with the service' was my final word in this exchange.

He himself seemed to be quite indifferent to money. Much later I visited him and his wife in their cottage. It was a winter evening and almost pitch dark. After we'd talked for a while by candle-light he picked up the only candle and, telling me he'd something he wanted to show me, led me up some rickety stairs to his workshop. This was littered with coffins and coffin lids, one of which he showed me with pride. It had a lot of figures scrawled on it in pencil, not easy to read by candlelight. 'This here', Syd said, 'has been sitting here since 1914. I always do my rough accounts on coffin lids. Somehow this one got hid away till just the other day. I thought you might be interested.' And I was. This particular account was for building a substantial brick wall and gate on the boundary between Poplar Farm and the road. It was addressed to Mr Wallace and had just been sent – forty-two years late – to his daughter, Mrs Gray. It demanded payment of £14 17s. 6d. and had been settled at once.

The Sharrett brothers had been responsible for building the Coffee Tavern which was a public meeting place where various organisations used to gather. It had two small meeting rooms downstairs and, above, a fair-sized billiard hall. The staircase connecting them was a wooden structure stuck curiously on to the back of the building. From the front it was quite a comely place but the back view was one which did no honour to the builder or the architect. With great glee Syd explained to me how this had come about. He'd been working for a few weeks on the site when he thought it was about time the architect came to inspect. The latter said he was too busy and quite trusted Mr Sharrett to be doing a good job. Syd tried once more to get him but met with the same reply. Finally he wrote to say the architect simply must come and do his final inspection as the building was completed according to the plans. The architect duly arrived and went over the ground floor with Syd, telling him he was very satisfied with everything. 'Now take me upstairs', says the architect.

'What stairs?' was Syd's reply.

'You has to go up a ladder and through a window same as we do. You didn't give us no stairs.'

Soon after our arrival in Eaton Bray I was elected to the diocesan youth committee and that led to my becoming the person with chief responsibility for the smooth running of the Easter Monday youth pilgrimage. This was a massive affair with young people coming from almost every parish in the diocese, converging in early afternoon on the Cathedral. The main body of pilgrims would assemble a mile away from the abbey and proceed together alongside the Verulamium lake and eventually into the nave which had been cleared of all chairs and pews except the choir stalls. In those days there were some three thousand pilgrims. Years later the numbers were to swell to over five thousand – a number too great to be entirely accommodated inside the abbey.

Our own young people of Eaton Bray were enthusiastic participants, walking the whole fifteen miles after a Communion service in church and breakfast in the vicarage. I couldn't walk with them as I had to be early in St Albans, marshalling the arriving groups and getting the procession started.

One of the first financial reforms needed, I saw, was the revenue from advertisements in the parish magazine. The production of this was entirely in my hands. On taking over I immediately decided to quadruple the charges for advertising and to improve the layout, ensuring that all ads were opposite reading matter except for the back cover, given over entirely to the advertisers. The printing was done in Leighton Buzzard, whither I went twice a month to cooperate with the printer in the production.

This wasn't the only area where I found that the Church had simply not moved with the times in assessing the value of things. Part of the vicar's stipend in those days came from glebe rents which had not been altered in the last fifty years. I visited my three glebe tenants and told them I intended as from the start of next year to charge them a proper economic rent. One said: 'About time too.' The other two argued the toss for a while; so I left them to think about it, saying they were of course free to give up their tenancies but the Church was no longer going to subsidise them. They both accepted the new terms.

The tenant who had been immediately ready for change was in fact the London Gliding Club. The secretary of the club wrote to me soon after all this asking if I would like to become an honorary member. I accepted with alacrity, visited the clubhouse and went gliding with one of their most experienced pilots, who told me they'd never had a fatal accident but they actually wanted to secure in perpetuity the land they were renting from me because if they ever lost it they would not have enough of a landing ground for complete safety.

Flying a glider was an amazing contrast to flying a Spitfire. The quiet, the gentle speed and the ever so gradual rate of descent were delightful to experience. The only moments I felt the least bit anxious were those in which we were getting airborne, towed by a Tiger Moth. Perhaps I was half remembering my previous experience of air towing in a Lysander with a drogue. The airfield was so placed on the edge of Dunstable Downs that there was nearly always a strong up-current which enabled one to stay up indefinitely in the immediate vicinity of the club.

One of the things I did not at first enjoy was chairing the Parochial Church Council (PCC). Its members always seemed to want to go on discussing matters that were not on the agenda and I didn't know how to keep them in order, being by far the youngest and least experienced person present. I had for a short time been on the PCC of St John's Church in Cambridge but I regretted having been forbidden by the dean to attend the meetings in St Albans Abbey Parish although I was an *ex officio* member.

I spent a fair bit of time trying to persuade the Council that the principal act of worship on Sunday should be the Eucharist, not Mattins or Evensong. I'd already made it a condition of accepting the living that I would after a year institute a Family Eucharist as the main Sunday service. Eventually they got to the point of telling me: 'For heaven's sake start the wretched thing and stop bleating about it.' This I declined to do, sticking to my plan of having a whole week's concentrated teaching in church given by a distinguished outsider before we began the new service. On the Saturday, the final day of this teaching week, which had been amazingly well attended, there were so many adverse comments that I was driven to demand: 'Who's going to be present at 9.30 tomorrow morning for our first Family Eucharist?' I got no reply and I lost my temper. I don't know what I said but remember I was very angry and then very ashamed of myself. We ended with a period of quiet prayer and saying the Grace together. I went home with a heavy heart.

Next morning there were three or four people at the 8 a.m. Communion, rather less than usual, then at 9.30 the church was almost full and fifty-one people communicated. So the battle was won and I suspect that my outburst of anger had helped work this wonder. A year later I was visiting Bert Bunker, who never failed to attend both Mattins and Evensong, when he said to me suddenly: 'Your service is all right, vicar.'

'What on earth do you mean?' I asked. 'You've never been to the Family Eucharist.'

'Ah, but I've seen the register', said Bert. 'Five pund six and tuppence and only two guineas at Mattins and we know who put that in.'

One day I was rung up by Hattie Gray to tell me that a certain woman in the village had died. So I set off at once to visit her bereaved husband, feeling sad that on this occasion I'd heard nothing about her illness, for sick visiting was my top pastoral priority. I got to the door and knocked. To my astonishment it was opened by the woman I'd been told was dead. 'Come in vicar', she said. 'Come and sit down. You look as if you'd seen a ghost.' She explained to me that she had been pretty poorly but evidently the news of her demise was greatly exaggerated and she was now fully recovered.

CHAPTER XXXI

Our garden at Eaton Bray was a lovely place for the children but it did cause us considerable anxiety on their behalf when we first saw it. Among its many attractions was what was known as the Moat – a large pond some eighty feet long and thirty-five feet wide. It was usually kept full by a water supply via a pipe that came from a stream which ran alongside Wallace's nurseries. The pond then would have some three or four feet of water but probably another six feet of mud under that. It was therefore essential to fence it round to ensure that none of our children fell in. From the pond flowed a stream in a deep ditch which seemed only slightly less dangerous than the pond itself. The stream eventually went into a pipe under our drive and came out fifty yards up the street where it rejoined the main stream from whence it had come.

To eliminate this danger I resolved to make another stream, which should run right on the edge of the lawn and be sufficiently attractive to make the stream in the ditch of no interest. To effect this I had to build a fairly substantial dam and thus raise the water level in the pond to the point where I could lead the overflow out into my newly dug streambed. My youngest brother, Martin, came to stay with us for a while when this work was in progress and did a great deal of the work with me. Unfortunately he used to bring even more mud into the house than I was apt to.

One of the other jobs that came my way was that the bishop appointed me an Inspector of Church Schools. I suppose this was on account of my little bit of teaching experience. It was a fascinating job. In one remarkable school at Little Gaddesden I was informed by the head teacher that the top class had been studying the 'synoptic problem', about which I myself had been blissfully ignorant until I went to Ely. I found the children were indeed able to tell me that Mark had written before the other Gospel writers who probably used him and another source called 'Q'.

Most of the other schools I inspected were vastly inferior but I did my best to be encouraging rather than negatively critical. It was when I got back from one of these inspections that I discovered that Sylvia was well into labour with our fourth child. I was able to join her for the birth which was as wonderful an experience as Rachel's had been. After this I put a notice on our drive gate telling the world that Sylvia had been successfully delivered of a son, Patrick.

Soon after we got settled in I started a Church youth club and was lucky enough not to have to carry much responsibility for its running. For most of our time we had one or other of two great leaders, John Lloyd, who also later became a churchwarden, and Bill Basham, who was our local bobby. He used to keep order among all the village youth by the simple expedient of a box around the ears if they were caught misbehaving. I was somewhat alarmed one youth club evening to find an agitated member at my front door asking me to come at once as they had been invaded by a large gang of motor cyclists from Luton who seemed intent on breaking the place up. I dressed up in my black cassock and cloak and went swiftly to the hall, outside which were parked some twenty motorcycles, and found the place full of aggressive looking youngsters. Mounting the stage and drawing myself up to my full six foot two I created silence apparently by my mere presence in that garb. I then said: 'All you non-members, GET OUT.' They filed out like lambs; the motorbikes started up and we were left in peace.

Later summer holidays were almost always spent at one or other of our parental homes. Having had one ancient Rover for one month for a summer holiday in Yorkshire I became aware that now we had four children it was actually cheaper to go by road than by rail. Once again I bought an old Rover; this one being much better than the earlier one. We decided to call her Mrs Binity. This was because this lady had been the subject of our Tony's curiosity for some time until one day he asked me, 'Who *is* Mrs Binity?' Neither Sylvia or I could at first discover what he was thinking about. Then one day while listening to a weather forecast Tony suddenly said: 'There you are. He said "Mrs Binity moderate to good"; and sometimes she's poor. Who is she?' We all hoped our Mrs Binity would be good for a long time to come. And she was. All the same we decided after a few years to buy a second-hand Bedford Workabus, which seated twelve and was thus able to carry virtually our whole choir when we went carol singing to the more remote parts of the parish.

We had several pretty cold winters, but our last one at Eaton Bray was by far the worst. In the depth of this 1963/64 winter we decided to abandon the use of our drawing room and turn the radiator off in the belief that this being the sunniest room in the house it ought to be able to survive on just the heat coming from an extra big pipe that went up the west wall from floor to ceiling. For some three days we never went into the room. When we finally did we found the radiator had burst and the carpet was covered in brown ice. I suppose it was lucky that the small pipe leading to the radiator was frozen solid. Meanwhile a radiator in the National School (now our church hall but retaining its old name) had also burst and a portion of it had actually hit and damaged the opposite wall. The explosion would have been highly dangerous had there been anybody present at the time.

This double mischance led me to discover what a wonderful insurance company we had in the Ecclesiastical. The diocese dealt with the damage in our house but it was the exploding radiator in the National School that the local Church had to pay for. I noted that the insurance policy specifically excluded burst pipes; so I wrote to say that we had suffered an explosion, which therefore was covered by our policy. I had a splendid letter back telling me that their legal experts assured them that what had happened to our radiator fell in the category of burst pipes not explosion. They would however give us an *ex gratia* payment which went a long way to paying for the new radiator.

Later on we had to deal with frozen pipes in our own attic and a fall of water and plaster through our bedroom ceiling. In the process of sorting this out our plumber managed to set the roof on fire with an exploding blow-lamp. At the same time he severely singed his eyebrows and was in a state of shock. While Sylvia attended to him I tore across to the church and grabbed the fire extinguisher which we had only recently acquired, and managed to put the fire out before much damage had been done.

To add to the miseries of this winter the vicarage fuel supply ran out and the coal merchant was unable to deliver us any more, though he told us we could go to the goods yard at Luton railway station and collect it ourselves. This we managed to do, getting two or three sacks full of anthracite and half thawed snow into the back of our workabus.

The first heavy snow fell that winter on Boxing Day. Roads all around us were blocked. We got chains fixed to our car wheels and still just managed to get about. However the main road between Edlesborough and Leighton Buzzard was completely blocked in one place where a double-decker bus got stranded and got snowed in so thoroughly that only the top of its roof showed above the snow-drift. I had to take a service in our neighbouring village of Whipsnade on one occasion and en route skidded violently, ending up facing the way I'd come.

Much of Whipsnade Zoo was actually in the Parish of Eaton Bray, including the four houses occupied by resident keepers. When I first learned this I thought it might enable me to take my children and odd guests into the zoo free of charge or at least at a reduced rate. With this in mind, in addition to my natural desire to get to know all my parishioners, I went one day to the entrance gate and asked permission to visit the keepers' families. 'Yer can't come in without yer pays', declared the keeper of the gate.

'Surely I'm entitled to visit my parishioners without paying', I countered. 'Nope', he said.

So I asked him to contact the top man and put my case to him. He disappeared inside his hut and a minute or so later returned: "E says its orlright fer yer to come in so long as yer doesn't look at no hanimals.'

'Do you want to blindfold me then and lead me by the hand?' I enquired, only to get the splendid reply: 'No. We trusts yer.'

That last winter went on and on. We were frozen up from Christmas right through to early March and apart from all the usual and extra duties imposed on me I found myself having to clear snow off the church roof and the paths in the churchyard. Our finances were at a low ebb and I used to sit in my study wearing extra pullovers and a greatcoat, only lighting the fire when I was expecting company. Of course the children loved it. We built snowmen and snow forts and our pond was obviously so thickly covered in ice that it was safe to use it as a skating rink. None of us had skates but a massive slide was created which gave endless fun especially to Michael and friends.

The 27 December was the anniversary of my parents' wedding. On that day my father presided at the altar of his little church in Matterdale, having been its curate for the five years since his retirement from the See of Brechin. This was his last service. After it he retired to bed, feeling incredibly weary. His heart was giving up and he had secondary cancers. I dashed up to see him and spent two days there, but felt I had to return to duty and all the winter problems at Eaton Bray. He died ten days later and we were relieved that he had been spared a long illness.

Out of the blue I got a letter from the bishop asking me if I would consider accepting the living of Harpenden. This wasn't in his gift but in that of the Lord Chancellor, who however paid a lot of attention to his recommendations. He added that he'd left me in peace a long time knowing that I wanted to minister in the country rather than in a town parish but now, he said, he thought my talents could be put to better use in what was one of the most prestigious parishes in the diocese and full of highly intelligent people including the staff of Rothamstead Agricultural Research Station. I confess that my heart sank at the prospect but it was certainly very flattering and after discussing it with Sylvia I agreed. Shortly after we were both summoned to meet the Lord Chancellor's Ecclesiastical Secretary at 10 Downing Street.

So to Downing Street we went, where we caught a brief glimpse of one of the Alex Douglas-Homes' daughters running upstairs and had an enjoyable exchange of views with Brigadier Watkins, the Ecclesiastical Secretary. A day or two after that we got the official letter inviting me to accept the living, which I did. When I telephoned my mother to give her the news I began by saying we'd just been to Downing Street. 'You're going to be a BISHOP!' she almost screamed at me in her delight. It hadn't crossed my mind that she might think like that. She was in the end fairly satisfied with the job I was going to.

CHAPTER XXXII

Harpenden was so different from Eaton Bray that I was only one among many who wondered if I would be up to the task of being its rector. The bishop had written a most flattering letter to the two excellent church-wardens, Henry Williamson and Peter Barclay, telling them how lucky they were to have me and that I would be teaching them how to pray better, which, he thought, was what the parish most needed after the amazingly efficient reorganisation that had been put in hand by my predecessor, Peter Bradshaw. The ministry of the laity was here a reality in a big way. The parish was divided into three sectors and each sector had its ARs (area representatives), whose task it was to take pastoral care of the folk in their area which could be as little as one road or as great as four or five. Each sector leader looked after his/her ARs and as in the days of Moses only the hardest cases were brought to the clergy, though they always visited the sick and house-bound.

There were lots of clergy. John Jones was Priest-in-Charge of All Saints, Peter Nott, though living in the central region of the parish church, was Priest-in-Charge of St Mary's, while John (Lord) Sandford, who was formerly in charge of that church, was now among the fairly large number of clerics whom we dubbed 'Floating Divines.' These were clergy who were either retired or who had non-parochial ministries and who were often called upon to take services for us and to help in other ways. With all this extra help we still needed an assistant curate at the parish church, a post which Peter Nott had held until the previous September. The bishop suggested I have Hilary Sharman who needed a move after four years in his previous parish. I never quite knew what he would do next but he was a trusted and loyal support. In particular he started straight away on a course in clinical theology at about the same time as Sylvia did.

My interest in this subject had begun in 1961 when at a clergy summer school Dr Frank Lake had been the main speaker over the whole four days of the school. He had made a tremendous impression and caused us to realise how desperately ill-equipped we were to deal with parishioners in mental or emotional distress. Even with a crowd of over two hundred clergymen he dared to teach experientially, demonstrating exactly what he was talking about and showing us a way of learning pastoral skills that went way beyond anything we were used to. On the last day of the school Frank asked those of us who wished to join one of his seminars to write our names on a list. The great majority of us did so and he had a hard task to whittle the numbers down to the twenty he reckoned he could take on. I was one of the lucky ones but had to undertake to become a tutor and teach others as soon as he, Frank Lake, said I was ready to.

Much of the teaching we received in our first year was of rather poor quality and barely experiential at all except when we had visits from Frank himself or from one of his psychiatric colleagues. In spite of that my enthusiasm remained high. I was shocked to be told by Frank before I had completed the two-year course that I was ready to start teaching the first-year syllabus. In fact it was only when I became a tutor that I really started to learn properly. This was because as tutors we had to attend residential conferences three times a year with Frank, when we would go carefully through the teaching ahead of us and learn by doing and by criticising each other. It was through Frank Lake, a psychiatrist, rather than from any of my theological teachers that I really took on board the meaning of that primary Pauline doctrine of justification by grace through faith. From him I learned that nobody, not even if abandoned by doctors as a hopeless case, was beyond the reach of a healing God acting through his well-trained clinical theologians. In a sense I had had some experience of this in my relationship with Herbert Blow. But now I was actually beginning to understand a great deal more about the neuroses which afflicted most people, none of whom, I learned, were normal. Normality belonged only to Jesus Christ, the one sinless – and therefore normal – human being.

The immediate result of all this was that people began coming to me for counselling. When we moved to Harpenden I was already tutor with a colleague to a seminar of some ten clergy, who all continued to come to our house after the move. On top of this I became increasingly involved in counselling of parishioners, which at first seemed to me a properly high priority.

What I ought to be doing and how to set about it were questions I had to answer and I decided to call in a management consultant who was a regular worshipper in the neighbouring parish and who therefore, I thought, should have a fair understanding of my work. He arrived by appointment, sat down and asked me: 'What is the Church for?' To which I blathered a bit and obviously had not got a ready answer. 'OK, rector,' he said, 'I'll see you again this time next week and perhaps you'll have an answer for me then. I can give you no advice until I know what you believe to be the purpose of the organisation for which you work.' With which wise words he departed.

Next week's interview started in the same way, only this time I gave him the answer he wanted, explaining at some length what I felt was the mission of the Church in general and in this parish in particular. 'Now,' he said, 'what is your job within this organisation?' To which I again blathered and indicated that I really didn't know. 'OK,' he said, 'back again next week.'

The following week we finally got started but the process couldn't get very far until I'd given him a complete time-and-motion study over a period of three weeks. This taught me that I spent an inordinate amount of time reading the paper, that I spent no less than forty hours a week on counselling or other talks with individuals and an average total of seventy-three hours' work each week. In order to marry my intentions with my actual behaviour I had to cut down on counselling and spend more time with groups and with my family. I don't think I was particularly successful in either of my cutting down areas but I did learn to spend more time with groups; indeed with Hilary Sharman's help I ran no less than four parochial clinical theology seminars. That at least meant that there was eventually a lot more counselling skill available in the parish. As these new seminars came into being I ceased doing any external tutoring but still regularly attended tutors' conferences with Frank Lake and thus enhanced my own understanding and skills. At Frank's suggestion I also embarked on a series of courses in group dynamics and in various psychotherapeutic systems such as *Gestalt* therapy and transactional analysis.

Among those serving the parish in a voluntary way the most outstanding was my secretary, Cornelia Clutterbuck. As a secretary she suffered from the grievous handicap of having no shorthand; but as an administrator she was invaluable. She always had a fierce loyalty to her rector, whether it were Peter Bradshaw or myself. She was a heavy smoker, highly strung, apt to blow her top with any fellow worker – and there were a vast number of these – wonderful with children, brilliant with her hands (she had built a massive brick wall in her own garden and was for ever making things for presents) and she wrote the greater part of the many administrative letters I had to sign each day. At first I did have to amend them a lot but she soon got used to my way of thinking and was able to compose most of them to my entire satisfaction.

Henry Williamson, who was chairman of a London catering company, was a wonderfully kind man. When we arrived he was nursing his long-time bedridden wife, which meant that he only did half a day's work each day in town. He still found time to help us settle in at the rectory and later to give me a guided tour of the sewage works, which were the pride and joy of the local Council, of which he was a leading member. Any stranger entering the parish church for a Sunday service would be almost sure to be met by Henry whose warmth towards all was palpable.

Harpenden was in fact full of wonderfully kind and generous people. In our nine years at Eaton Bray, much enjoyed as they were, we were invited out to meals less than half a dozen times. Now at Harpenden everyone seemed to want to entertain us. We had moved into a totally different environment; we had almost doubled our income; we had found immensely stimulating company all round us; and on top of all this it was clear that such gifts as I had were going to be used to the full.

This parish was the richest I've ever come across. I don't mean simply in terms of money, though that also was true, but in its talents of every kind. In addition to all the boffins of Rothamstead we had many of the top civil servants and not a few captains of industry. We were also rich in theologians. Gordon Wakefield, at that time in charge of Methodism's Epworth Press with the title of Connexional Editor, became a close friend. He was later to be a district chairman and later still a canon of Lichfield, I think the only Methodist ever to be given an anglican canonry. Then there was Ulrich Simon, lecturer in Divinity at King's College, London, who caused me great wonder when he borrowed from me Frank Lake's magnum opus *Clinical Theology*, a book of some half a million words full of technical psychiatric as well as theological terms and accompanied by the most amazingly complicated charts representing all kinds of psychological disturbance and their provenance. He came back ten days later to say he'd found it most inspiring and thought-provoking but could I spend some time with him explaining the charts – the only part of the book which he found difficult.

These were the days of the Cold War. One day a senior civil servant told me: 'If the Russians wanted to knock this country out, all they'd have to do would be to drop an old-fashioned atom bomb on Harpenden on a Sunday afternoon, and we'd be finished.' He meant of course that most of the people who really ran the country were the civil service chiefs who would be taking their ease here at the weekend.

Almost as great a concern was the situation in South Africa. Harpenden was massively conservative and although many people still thought of the Church of England as the Conservative Party at prayer, I was a Liberal in politics. So when the British government, in spite of the general dislike of the apartheid regime, was still supplying the South African government with armoured cars I joined in a demonstration organised in Harpenden as in many other places, wearing a black head-dress and parading up and down the main street carrying placards denouncing 'arms for South Africa'. I suspect that it was actions of mine like this that made it necessary for the Church to appoint safer people to follow me whenever I changed jobs. Two of them became bishops and one became one of our most famous archdeacons – George Austin, who was ever ready to speak up for the conservative traditionalists of the Church of England.

CHAPTER XXXIII

The move from Eaton Bray was well timed for all our boys but not good for Rachel, who suffered all the usual strains of being the parson's daughter as well as those deriving from joining a new school at the top end of it. Worse still the head teacher had told her she must appear fully kitted out in the official uniform, whereas she found to her dismay that she was the only girl in her class so doing. Michael was off to his College of Education at Padgate, where he found himself using the same buildings as I'd briefly occupied when they were part of a transit camp in the war. Tony quickly settled in at the Francis Bacon School in St Albans, which specialised in music and where he shone. Patrick was happy enough to transfer from the village school but, as the rector's son and the godson of the Deputy Head, David Warner, had a rotten time at St Nicholas' School, Harpenden. He later moved on to St George's, which was a very good school, co-educational but in many ways more like a public school than a state school. Here he met Eric Morecambe, whose daughter was a pupil and who was as amusing a character in private life as he was on stage with Ernie Wise. Like Eric, we all supported Luton Town FC and once Patrick got a lift with him en route for the Saturday match.

At Padgate Michael soon met and started courting Jill Moore, who came from Ramsgate in Kent. He started the habit, adopted by all three of our sons, of falling for very small women. Our sons were all around six foot tall and those various girlfriends we got to know hardly ever came within ten inches of them. Michael and Jill got married in the summer of 1967 and I tied the knot for them.

Harpenden had its own cottage hospital known as the 'Red House', of which I was chaplain. I was still actively engaged in the ministry of healing and spent probably rather too much time with the sick. On one occasion I was summoned late in the evening by the Matron to a patient who, she told me, was going to die that night. Matron was a devout Roman Catholic and the patient was a friend of hers but not a Catholic. She hoped I could do for him whatever an Anglican priest could do for the dying. When I got to him he did indeed look near his end but he agreed to let me minister to him. When I had prayed and laid hands on him for healing, blessed him and left the hospital, I didn't expect to see him again. I popped in for a few minutes next day and found him sitting up in bed, looking and feeling perfectly well. They kept him in for a further few days under observation; after which he was discharged. The big surprise in this case was that a few weeks later I was about to pass him in the street. He looked up and, as soon as he saw me, crossed rapidly to the other side of the road taking good care not to look at me.

My own inner life was still fairly exciting. When I look back to that time I'm aware that I was almost certainly a little manic. This meant that I could sometimes overwork to the extent that my body simply collapsed. Twice this happened rather dramatically and each time wise superiors insisted on my taking some sick leave. When this happened at Harpenden we were given £100 by my archdeacon and another £100 by the PCC and so we went off for a fortnight to Cornwall and gorged ourselves on good food and great scenery.

On Maundy Thursday we always had an evening Sung Eucharist followed by an all-night vigil of prayer. Holy Week was a very busy time with extra services, long readings and not a few addresses.

One year when I was well into the Maundy Thursday Eucharist, presiding at the altar, I realised that though I had thought a bit about a sermon on the meaning of 'the blood of Christ', I hadn't actually found time to sit down and write one out as my practice always was. However it was one of those days when I really felt high on God and as I stood at the altar I simply felt I was floating with no contact with the floor.

The time came for me to preach and I sailed down to the pulpit, ascended the steps without feeling them, opened my mouth and preached. I've no idea what I said but am sure it was brilliant, the best I'd ever done because I had nothing to do with the composing of it. I was speaking words which just arrived out of the blue, coming I assumed from the Holy Spirit, from God. How I wish they could have been recorded! I would like to know if this was all a delusion or, as I much prefer to think, a genuine gift from Heaven. Before I left the pulpit I glanced down and noticed a stool at its foot. This struck me as odd for some reason although there was nothing unusual about its position.

Only gradually as the service moved towards its conclusion did I feel I was down to earth again. Saying goodnight to the congregation afterwards one woman took me aside, having waited until the crowd had left, and said: 'Did you know you levitated during the service?'

'Well, I know I felt my head was in the clouds and my feet hardly on the ground for some of the time', I confessed. This parishioner was psychic; she saw auras and puzzled me a lot. I'd visited her house in the depths of winter. She was a widow living alone. As soon as I entered the house I found it was very cold and she hastened to put on an electric fire for me. She herself didn't need any artificial heat, never used her central heating or even a local heater except when she had company. I was convinced of her genuineness and it was because of her that I joined the local branch of the Churches' Fellowship for Psychical and Spiritual Study (CFPSS).

That Maundy Thursday night after talking to this woman I went back to the pulpit, saw that the stool still stood in its proper place in front of it, mounted the steps and looked down. From that position the stool was invisible because of the bookstand on the front edge of the pulpit. I worked out that I'd have to have been about two feet taller to have seen the stool while preaching. As far as I know nobody else saw anything odd during the service but the observation of the psychic, added to my own experience, convinced me that something strange had really happened and I wasn't simply going round the bend.

I remember very little now about what I learned from the CFPSS but one thing was that we all have three bodies – the material, the astral and the spiritual; and I may have got that wrong! My theory at least is that my consciousness during that episode moved from my material to my astral body, so that I could see what I knew to be there although it was out of range of my material eyes. This seemed to account for the fact that a psychic woman could see what my astral body was doing. I don't for a moment believe that a photograph would have at any time revealed anything unusual about me. I can't help wondering whether this experience of mine was more or less the same as the 'genuine' cases of levitation recorded in the lives of some saints.

In February 1970, Michael Gresford-Jones having retired, we got a new bishop – Robert Runcie, whom I had already met at Cuddesdon. Soon after his enthronement he invited me to sit at the right hand of Archbishop Michael Ramsey who was to dine with him at Abbey Gate House in the company of the whole Bishop's Council. I arrived in good time and was met at the door by Lindy, our new bishop's wife. She was a concert pianist but she was also a keen gardener with lots of plans for her new garden. She told me she'd heard I was a keen gardener and took me off at once on a guided tour of their spacious grounds, telling me about her plans at length and in detail; in all of which I was very interested. The time slipped by very pleasantly until suddenly a stentorian voice hailed her from the terrace. It was her husband, proclaiming: 'The archbishop and Mrs Ramsey have been here for ten minutes – and no hostess. What have you been doing?' Lindy told him exactly what she'd been doing. This gave me a quick insight into the stupid stuff some people in the media were to churn out about the Runcie marriage. I thought it was wonderful and most inspiring to the many less brave clergy wives who were expected to live their lives as unpaid curates or personal assistants to their husbands. That old tradition did sometimes work well but many clergy marriages must have been terribly strained by such ridiculous expectations.

I knew the archbishop had just visited both Canada and South Africa; so there was plenty to talk about. He told me that one of his problems in Capetown was that he had resolved never to smile in the presence of Dr Verwoerd, the South African President. Since Michael Ramsey spent most of his life smiling at people this must have been very difficult for him. He told me he'd been fooled by the press too often to make them a gift of a smile in the presence of that hateful man. He had triumphantly succeeded in looking grim every time he was snapped in the President's company but was his usual smiling self in the company of black church folk.

Bob Runcie was a better theologian than his predecessor, who read widely and wisely but relied on his canon theologian, Murdoch Dahl, to be the chief diocesan thinker. The most striking statement our new bishop made in a talk given at his first clergy summer school with us was that Jesus was a man transparent to God. He thus gave us a clear picture of his own answer to Christ's question: 'What think ye of Christ?' I've never come across a better one.

I had a wonderful lot of assistant curates. In addition to John, Peter and Hilary there were Ian Robson, Frank Mitchinson and then Roger Davis at All Saints, David Ireland at St Mary's, and Kenith David and Peter Cianchi at the parish church. Each brought his distinctive gifts and I learned something from all of them.

In the winter of 1970/71 Sylvia was suffering and for a long time I failed to notice this. Matters came to a head when we treated ourselves to a trip up to London to see *West Side Story*: a marvellous experience but one that was temporarily marred by what followed. When we got to St Pancras the last train to Harpenden was almost ready to start and, grabbing her hand, I made Sylvia run with me to catch it. She was completely exhausted by this and I still didn't realise that she was ill. When next day she did see our doctor he quickly diagnosed her severe anaemia and told me I might have killed her by what I had done.

Soon she was in the care of University College Hospital in London, where blood transfusions and drip feeding eventually gave way to surgery. A total hysterectomy did eventually solve her problems but she was left very weak and needed plenty of tender loving care after she got home; and the getting home couldn't have been much worse, for having gone to collect her myself, the car broke down when we were not quite half-way home and we'd got pretty cold by the time we were rescued. Back in Harpenden between two stays in UCH an angel of mercy in the shape of Greta McClean, the wife of our GP's senior partner, invited Sylvia to come and stay in their house for as long as she wanted, to be nursed and cosseted. Nothing could have been better for her. The McCleans were always the most hospitable of people and it was well nigh impossible to visit Sylvia there without having a spot to drink and pleasant and lively conversation with her hosts.

Soon after this I severely damaged our old Vauxhall and the garage said it was beyond repair. Our Michael's father-in-law, Roy Moore, then asked me if I'd like to have his old Jaguar. I said I certainly would and we agreed to accept the valuation made by his Ramsgate garage as the amount I'd pay him. The value was put at £230 but Roy then had the car completely overhauled so that when I picked it up it was like new. I loved this car, a Mark II, like that driven by Inspector Morse. Its maintenance costs were surprisingly low because I found a garage in Harpenden which dealt solely with Jags and the proprietors charged me only half their normal rate. This wasn't only because I was the rector but chiefly because I always paid my bills as soon as the job was done whereas their other clients used to keep them waiting anything up to two years for their money. On top of this one of our parishioners, David Hubbard, was an engineer who, as part of his Christian commitment, volunteered to carry out all minor services to the cars of all the parish clergy.

One day not long after acquiring my Jag I was driving at sixty miles per hour down the A6 when I saw, riding on the wide grass verge, a horse ridden by a teenage girl. As I approached, the horse suddenly reared and backed out into the road in front of me. There was a stream of traffic coming towards me but luckily nothing immediately behind me; so, breaking hard, I swerved out as far as I dared, so that the horse, when it hit me, didn't cause a smash. It did however do quite a lot of damage to the car, which ended up with a large dent adorned with a long strip of horse-hair glued to it. I pulled up on the grass verge and walked back to see what the damage was to the other party. The girl, who was about fourteen, was a bit shaken but unhurt. The horse had a great scorch mark round its rump but seemed otherwise all right.

The lass said it was entirely her fault and she was going to be in terrible trouble because she'd borrowed the horse on the strict understanding that she was to stick to the fields and on no account to go on the road. She gave me her own name and address and those of the owner, whom I 'phoned as soon as I got home. The owner said I wasn't to worry. She took complete responsibility and the horse was comprehensively insured; so I could go ahead and get the car repaired and send the bill to her insurers.

The bill came to £50 but the insurers then told me that owing to the law of *scienter* they were not liable. I asked one of the solicitors in my congregation whether he would like to take the case up for me. He said he would be thrilled to do it and it might go all the way to the House of Lords. The law of *scienter*, he told me, simply meant that a man was assumed to have more sense than a horse; and since the horse in question was being ridden by a minor without the consent of the owner, it might well be presumed that the horse could be regarded as riderless and if that were so the law of *scienter* would certainly apply. It was what he termed a 'nice case' but, as my friend, his advice was not to pursue it because insurance companies very seldom lost their cases.

Before we left Harpenden, I had built in the Rectory garden my second most elaborate pingway (see Chapter XXX). The track ran from the balcony above our sunroom across to a massive beech tree and thence above our roadside fence with various points and alternative routes, all of which met finally to discharge the golf balls via a pipe running below ground onto the paving just below their starting point. Passers-by in the road used to look up in amazement when the pingway was in use, seeing these golf balls travelling on virtually invisible wires some twenty feet above the pavement.

CHAPTER XXXIV

In spite of all efforts to prevent it the number of severely disturbed parishioners who came to me for counselling steadily increased, so that I began to think the only solution was to move to another job. Sometimes the problems were dealt with well enough, but at others, particularly in the realm of depression, we could not reach a happy outcome. In fact within two years of my departure three of my former clients had taken their own lives.

I was thinking like this when I received a letter from Christopher Pepys, Bishop of Buckingham who was an old Cuddesdon student from my father's days, inviting me to become Vicar of Aylesbury or at least to come and talk to him about it and have a look at the parish. So I drove over. Christopher was impressed by my car, he being a very keen and very fast driver. He demonstrated his skill as he drove me round Aylesbury, glimpsing bits of my future domain. I was unfavourably impressed. The vicarage was nothing like as pleasant a house as Harpenden Rectory; the church was vast, gloomy and cold. The old town centre had been destroyed. Most of the parish consisted of vast London overspill housing estates. There was a daughter church of St Peter on one of these estates and an excellent curate, Dan Richards to look after it. There were three hospitals, of which the vicar was chaplain. Aylesbury was the county town. The tradition of the parish church of St Mary was Anglo-Catholic but the place was almost dead. The only signs of life I could spot were the organist, Des Harvey, and his choir, and Elliott Viney, churchwarden and undisputed senior layman.

When I got home I told Sylvia all about it. My own feeling was that I didn't want to go but maybe was meant to. So we soon went together to have another and more thorough look. This time we met Canon Byard, who was just retiring after twenty-seven years as vicar. He had an unfortunate impediment in his speech, which was so severe as to make him unintelligible to Sylvia and obviously to many other people. Perhaps because I was a linguist I found that with difficulty I could follow what he said. The gist of it was that everything in the parish was in a bad way now except for the fabric of the church itself. Just before we left the vicarage he informed me that I would be absolutely the wrong person to succeed him.

The house, like the church, was filthy. Walking down the passage from the hall to the kitchen I surreptitiously slid my thumbnail along the wall removing thereby a strip of dirty grease. Outside the kitchen window was a pile of tea-leaves reaching up to the sill. The garden was full of sycamore trees. The study was so dark that even in summertime it needed to be lit artificially. The drawing room ceiling had a large brown patch on it above the place where the canon obviously sat and smoked his pipe.

Sylvia thought, if possible, even less of the prospect than I did; nor were we in the least surprised to hear that two other priests had already turned it down. She did in the end agree with a letter I composed and sent to Bishop Pepys, which was, I supposed, as good as a refusal. It ran something like this:

> Having given the matter a great deal of thought and with my wife's full approval, I am willing to put out a kind of Gideon's fleece. We don't want to come to Aylesbury but are aware that it might be the will of God that we do so. The conditions on which I would accept the living are these:
>
> The stipend to be increased by £300 per annum.
>
> The expenses allowance be increased from £50 to £500 per annum.
>
> A new window be built in the study in the wall facing the street.
>
> A shower room be created in addition to the bathroom.
>
> The central heating system be expanded so that it is total rather than partial.
>
> The house be redecorated from top to bottom.

By return of post came a letter from the bishop saying, 'Congratulations, vicar designate. Your conditions are accepted.'

So that was it. We had to go. The contrast between Harpenden and Aylesbury could hardly have been greater. People who didn't know the current scene thought of Aylesbury as a picturesque old market town. The reality was very different. Around the great church of St Mary was a cathedral-type close but this was now a centre for drug distribution and vandalism. Whereas in Harpenden the clean and compact church was always open except at night, St Mary's, Aylesbury was locked except at service times and there were always broken windows because they couldn't be repaired as fast as they were broken by yobs hurling stones through them.

Over the road from the vicarage garden was a Labour Club, which was the venue for extremely boisterous parties every Saturday night, which usually ended after midnight when numerous drunks would be shouting and singing round the place. When we finally arrived we were greeted by a dead dog which had been thrown over the wall into our garden.

The garden too was a contrast to the one we were used to. Everything in it was unkempt. Sycamore seedlings were everywhere; there was a weedy lawn and a weed-filled flowerbed almost hid a lovely old wall behind it. In the area just outside the kitchen I planned where I would clear away the soil and put in a drain and build a retaining wall. I could see that there were possibilities, as of course there always are. The place was like the parish. Both the bishop and Elliott Viney had told me: 'Do anything you like with this place. Anything is bound to be better than what went before.'

Among my early counselling contacts were a woman who murdered a baby, a heroin addict who took his own life and a grave-robbing self-styled black magician.

Before we left Harpenden I was visited by John Waller, who had been offered the living. John had been a year junior to me at Teddy's and already had experience as a team rector. I was delighted that he was to succeed me in this great parish and took great pleasure in briefing him on it. Leaving our numerous friends was a sad business. The move was made on the last day of 1972. We found the central heating had been attended to and worked well. The powers that be had not agreed to everything the bishop had promised; so we had to pay for the shower ourselves. The redecoration had barely started and it was to be three months before the painter finally left us in sole occupation. The PCC had agreed to pay my greatly increased expenses allowance but on studying the finances I wasn't sure they'd be able to.

Canon Byard had told me the finances were in order and that the church had recently been thoroughly overhauled. This turned out to be a less than wholly accurate statement. The fabric fund had less than £100 in it. The building, massively restored by Gilbert Scott a century before, had been tinkered with and often inexpertly repaired with mortar used that was harder than the stones it was supposed to cement. It had a central heating system designed for a coke-fired boiler but now fired by oil. The system was totally closed, with no expansion tank or safety valve except on the boiler itself, which was at least thermostatically controlled but this meant that whenever it switched itself on or off the whole pipework had to expand or contract; which it did with enormous bangs. To be in church while the heating was on was like being on a battlefield. One would be aware of what seemed like occasional sniper fire interrupted by explosions as of a hand-grenade. It was hardly surprising that the congregation had dwindled to near vanishing point.

Some time before my institution as vicar an article appeared in the local paper which was chiefly an interview with Bishop Pepys, in which he said that he'd appointed someone who would put Aylesbury on the map church-wise. While I'd no doubt this was true, I felt it was a less than tactful thing to publish where all Aylesbury could read it, including my predecessor who had retired to the neighbouring village of Stoke Mandeville. He'd been vicar since the end of the Second World War; and at that time the congregation of St Mary's had been largely made up of ladies and gentlemen who drove in from the villages round about. In 1945 there had been over 350 Easter Communicants. Now hardly anyone came from outside the town and there was an underlying hostility to the Church, which it took me several years to understand.

Aylesbury had been a parliamentary stronghold in the Civil War but the Church had stood out for Charles I. It had been used for all kinds of non-Church purposes, including the stabling of royalist horses and as the law court. There had even been a gallows in the churchyard, where an adolescent had been hanged for sheep-stealing within the memory of grand-parents of some of the current oldest inhabitants. Since even in the twentieth century St Mary's had been the place of worship favoured by the 'oppressive class', it was hardly surprising that the 'oppressed' shunned it.

The pattern of worship I inherited was the same as had been the case when I got to Eaton Bray but the attendance was smaller. In a building that could seat 1,500 people it was a brave person who would join such a tiny congregation. At my first 8 a.m. Communion service I found myself facing eastwards at the High Altar with one server the only person within earshot. The rest of the congregation – about twenty strong – was scattered around the vast nave stretching back to the west wall some sixty yards away behind my back.

At the 11 o'clock Mattins we had the choir which did a good job but apart from it there was only a handful of worshippers. Six o'clock Evensong was similar. All the services were from the 1662 Book of Common Prayer. I found the whole experience intensely depressing and resolved to get everything changed.

With the cooperation of the churchwardens we arranged to cut-off the western half of the nave by placing umbrella stands across the aisles. This ploy failed for, to my amazement, the folk who favoured the back row still went and sat there, climbing over the obstacles we'd designed to prevent this.

Exacerbating the problem was the fact that I was beginning to have difficulty in hearing even under better conditions. Tests showed that I was quite seriously hearing-impaired, as my family had been telling me for some time. My hearing loss was due, the experts told me, to a big bang quite a long time ago.

Even before my institution I'd visited the Council offices and made the acquaintance of the Mayor and her Secretary Doug Joss who had been a Squadron Leader in the RAF and to whom I owe an enormous debt of gratitude. He said there were two things he could do for me: first, he could get me going to a tribunal to claim compensation for my war injuries, my hearing loss, my back injury and my arm injury; and then he got me writing to the appropriate authority to get my war medals, which I'd never thought about at the time when I was busy adjusting to freedom, marriage, university and civvy street.

For the tribunal I had to have another hearing test, which was carried out at Stoke Mandeville Hospital. The consultant said he'd no doubt at all that my big bang was the cause of my trouble and that this particular kind of hearing loss would get steadily worse. His prognosis was that with luck I'd still have a little hearing by the time I was seventy but if I lived long enough I would inevitably become really deaf. I then acquired from the NHS my first hearing aids which took some getting used to but certainly helped me.

The tribunal was held in Oxford. At the end of it the chairman informed me that I would be hearing from the War Pensions Agency officially but he could tell me at once that I would certainly get a substantial pension backdated to the day on which I'd applied to be heard; and, much more importantly, that I would always be entitled to the best hearing aids available in Britain at the government's expense. Thirty years before I'd thought myself extremely lucky not only just to be alive, but also to have recovered the use both of my arm and of my ears. Of course I was lucky and also delighted to be getting a pension but the prospect of getting steadily deafer was not appealing. My hearing loss did make a profound difference to my life. I was very much in the business of human relationships and those relationships are much more difficult when you cannot hear more than half of what other people are saying to you.

On several occasions I thought seriously about taking early retirement but always, just in time, some better hearing aids would come on the market and, though they were not always available to all comers on the NHS, I was able to obtain them as promised, even if at times this required many letters and the intervention of my MP.

One of the most depressing things about the church was that on the rare occasions when some brave mother brought a child to a service several members of the congregation would be sure to turn and scowl at the child. So I took to telling young parents when I was out visiting that they would be well advised not to bring a child to St Mary's before I told them it would be safe to do so. It was a great delight to me that before so very long I was able to get in touch with all these parents and give them the all clear. After this several did dare to come along with children and gradually the 9.30 became a real family service.

CHAPTER XXXV

While at Harpenden I'd started going on numerous educational courses to learn more about my job. I kept actively involved in clinical theology and also in the study of leadership and the dynamics of groups. Though the new job at Aylesbury was very demanding of my time, I felt I simply must keep up this regime of ongoing learning. I discovered that in the average year I secured grants from the diocese for these courses which used up one-third of what was available for all the clergy of Buckinghamshire. Since so few people were interested, the bishop was glad to authorise these grants for me.

One result of my new learning was that I decided to set up a Growth Group. I got eight volunteers including both Dan Richards and Sylvia. The idea of the group was simply to meet and tell the truth in love about how we felt about the group and anything else that cropped up. The first meeting could easily have been a disaster. One of the members, an elderly woman who was very brave to have come at all, burst into tears at one point on discovering that one or two members of the group actually thought she was loveable. At the end of the meeting four of its members told me they wouldn't be coming any more. During the following week I visited each of them on their own and having been able to convince them that the weeping had been caused by joy not distress and had been thoroughly beneficial for the weeper, they all agreed to come back for the next session. Once we'd had a good look at our normal ways of concealing our feelings and learned that it was actually better to have them listened to we got on much better.

The new life that began to spring up in the parish came almost entirely from this and other small groups. I had learned that effective group work depended on attention being paid to three elements: the individual needs of the members, the maintenance of the health of the group itself and finally the task in hand. On my arrival in Aylesbury I'd been approached by a group of people who were looking for a meeting place in which to study the subject of the Church and Community Development. This place I gladly provided and I also joined the group, with whom I sharpened up a lot of rather incoherent thoughts which in due time led to the beginnings of the Community Project at St Mary's. At every opportunity I sought to get people to ask themselves the basic question that had been put to me by that management consultant in Harpenden: 'What is the Church for?' I think I was able to persuade many people that Archbishop William Temple had it exactly right when he said, 'The Church is, as far as I know, the only major institution which exists for the benefit of those who do not belong to it.'

Once a number of people within the parish had more or less come to accept that principle the next question was, 'What do we do with the church building?' We had inherited this vast place, full of history going back to the thirteenth century and it seemed obviously crazy to suppose its best use was for a tiny gathering of aged Christians to meet on Sundays while for the rest of the time it remained cold and empty and for most of the day actually locked up.

I so hated being responsible for a locked church that I disregarded all the advice I was given and decided to leave it unlocked for most of the day. I was in there at least twice and often three or four times a day but could not prevent the ensuing vandalism. One day when I went in I found someone had split the spines of all the hymn books. Even more distressing, though less costly, on another occasion I discovered that someone had decided to shit in the font, which dating back to 1180 was one of the most valuable and interesting possessions of the church.

That made me give in – but only for a breather. I next tried to organise a rota of church-watchers, people who would come and simply sit, read, pray or patrol around so that would-be vandals would be deterred. I'd not expected this to be controversial but it was. A letter attacking the idea and its author was published in the local paper, comparing me unfavourably with Canon Byard, who was said always to have kept the church unlocked, frequently visited by himself and who, unlike me, was a regular visitor in the hospitals.

The volunteers materialised in sufficient numbers to have the church open for most of the day for almost the whole week, though the scheme did not get completed before the catastrophic event that got us started on the long road to a more glorious future. In August 1974 one of the massive nave pillars developed a split of alarming proportions. As soon as I'd seen it and with the blessing of the churchwardens I dashed out to the old ruined church at Hartwell, some five minutes' drive away, which I knew was being lovingly restored. I asked the stone mason working there if he would come with me and advise me what to do about our problem. He came at once and it seemed to me that the crack in that pillar had got wider while I'd been away.

His advice, which we followed speedily, was to strap it with planks held together by wire ropes. By the time we got this done a second pillar had begun to split. So we gave it the same treatment. Our mason had told me that he certainly wouldn't sleep a night in the church for all the tea in China. He also told us that as a matter of urgency we should get scaffolding up to take the weight of the roof off these pillars, which we then got on with repairing and strengthening. That cost us a mere £8,000 but the survey done next by our architect revealed that we needed to spend over £100,000 simply to make the church safe and sound.

Of course I knew that we also had to replace the heating system and the lighting and that the organ needed a rebuild. In spite of all that had happened there was such a conservative mood among many of our people that radical solutions seemed to them unnecessary. Indeed Wilf Harman, later himself to become churchwarden and a wonderful friend to me, told me he didn't see why we should be worried. 'This church has stood for seven hundred years', he said, 'and I can't see it falling down now.'

The congregation was still very small, the financial reserves were virtually nil and though we had staved off the total collapse of St Mary's the outlook was bleak. We investigated the possibility of getting the church or at least part of it declared redundant. We thought we might keep just the chancel for worship and either demolish or sell off the rest. We sought the cooperation of all the other major local Churches with the idea that a restored St Mary's might be shared among the lot of us. Though they all had problems with their buildings none wished to amalgamate. Next door to the church was the fine Prebendal House, which had just ceased to be a Girls' School – indeed the school to which our daughter Rachel had belonged after leaving Eaton Bray school. I had ambitions about the churches of Aylesbury acquiring this too; but nobody was willing to put up the money. Nor were the Church Commissioners, to whom I made a tentative approach. They did however send someone down to look at our problems.

My meeting with him was cordial and constructive but it left me with a massive responsibility. In short their decision was that I must do everything in my power to effect a complete restoration of the building before any other alternative would be considered.

Until the end of 1975 the St Mary's congregation lived in a kind of limbo but there were signs of more life among the ruins. Then came the final blow to our tottering building. On 2 January 1976 we were hit by a massive gale – quite the most terrifying storm I'd ever experienced. At its height that evening we went to our front door and glanced out, worried because our Tony and Patrick were somewhere out in the town. Tiles and slates were hurtling through the air, branches were breaking off trees. The racket was terrific. We withdrew hastily. Next an almighty crash came and we thought our house was falling down. A mass of brickwork came tumbling out of our drawing room fireplace and outside the window we could see the tallest of our chimneys embedded in our lawn.

Tony and Patrick got home unscathed and apart from a large hole in the roof and a fair number of tiles gone missing we didn't personally suffer much more. In the morning however when I went over to the church things were much more serious. The western parapet of the tower had been blown in. Miraculously none of the massive stones had toppled over the edge but a number of smaller pieces had fallen the twenty-five or thirty feet down to the nave roof. Even before this the roof had leaked and it was not improved by the night's events. We got a small party of men together and went up the tower and carefully tied ropes round each of the massive fallen stones and then tied the lot to a rope encircling the central spirelet.

There followed discussions with the local authority about the safety of the building, which at first they thought should be closed. In the end we reached a compromise and, shutting off the whole of the nave, we were allowed to use the chancel and a side chapel for worship.

My next step was to secure the cooperation of the County Council's chief officers and in particular those involved with education, youth and community, and social services in the project which was to lead to St Mary's becoming a Community Centre as well as a place of worship. I got the whole-hearted backing of Simon Burrows, our new Bishop of Buckingham after I'd sufficiently researched the history of St Mary's to demonstrate that it had been used for many secular purposes over the centuries.

We decided to appeal for £175,000 towards the architect's estimate of

Opposite.   Main Photo: The scaffolding installed.
  Insets: The first crack discovered;
                        Making the pillar safe;
                        Chaos.

£225,000 for the whole work, believing that we could find £50,000 from the sale of assets and a charity which was intended to maintain the clock and its chimes. In order to raise this sum we employed a professional fundraiser and a committee of volunteers headed by Reg Maxwell who was Clerk to the Borough Council. We had almost raised it by the time the planned restoration and reordering was completed in March 1979 but by then we knew there was still a lot more that needed to be done over the next few years. But the basic job was complete in time for a rededication service on 9 May, which was a magnificent affair with massive representation of Church and State and a congregation of about a thousand people. In that month's issue of the *Oxford Diocesan Magazine* we had a cover picture of the reordered church with the heading 'The Aylesbury Miracle' and a two-page illustrated article by the editor inside.

During the restoration it was of course impossible to use the church at all. We therefore had our weekday services and meetings in the vicarage and for Sundays had an arrangement with the High Street United Reformed Church, by which we had our Family Eucharist at 9.30, the URC had their morning service at 11.00 and we combined in the evening with the service being URC one Sunday and C of E the next. The theory was that we would in due time make St Mary's available to the URC just as they'd shared their building with us. This was because they'd had a wonderful offer for their very valuable premises which they felt they couldn't refuse and they hoped to build a better and up-to-date church with a nice endowment fund available as well. It never worked out like that and I suspect that some members of the URC were very happy to see the last of us. This was largely because we had a lot of children, some of whom used to drop sweet papers about the place. Possibly also their leadership was not amused when we returned to St Mary's, taking their organist and several other members with us.

For my part I found the whole experience useful and I quite enjoyed preaching in the combined evening service at twice the length I'd ever gone to with an all-Anglican congregation. Weekday Communion services round our dining table in the vicarage were greatly appreciated by people who had never before attended such informal acts of worship. I was glad to be

Opposite. Main Photo: The interior of St Mary's, Aylesbury.
Photograph by Graham Jeffery.
Inset: St Mary's, Aylesbury.
Photograph by Mary Farnell.

able to preside over these without the dressing up that was obligatory in church.

I think I grew a lot more liberal and less stuffy at this period; and in this I was much helped by a splendid curate, Bernard Metcalfe, who challenged many of my Anglo-Catholic assumptions. He was also quite invaluable on our planning committee, where his architectural training was used to the full. One of his greatest ideas was the construction of our movable octagonal podium on which the central altar was to stand, enabling us with very little furniture shifting to have worship in the round or in the traditional way with the altar at the east end of the nave and the congregation seated in straight rows facing it. Personally I came to love the 'in the round' setting which was based on the same principles as had inspired the Roman Catholic Liverpool Cathedral.

Among those who made the 'miracle' happen several people were of enormous importance. Peter Burridge, whose wife Isabelle was for a time my splendid secretary, did a wonderful job in teaching the principles of Christian Stewardship and running our first campaign. Peter Symonds, a brilliant all-rounder, was a quantity surveyor who probably saved us many thousands of pounds and ensured that all the work done was of top quality. He and his wife Sheila became close friends of ours and we were truly shattered when, his great work for the restoration just completed, he was killed in the Clapham railway accident. Elliott Viney was a tower of strength because he was an historian who knew St Mary's better than anyone else and could have made life very hard for us if he'd not been whole-heartedly in support of what we were planning. John Bush, who lived in St Mary's Square but initially divided his Church loyalties between us and his nearby home village, was for me what Lt Bush was to Captain Hornblower. He led and trained a group of servers and worked tirelessly behind the scenes in a worship committee we set up and in many other ways. He wanted to be accepted for ordination and in my view would have been a totally reliable and excellent priest. I think he was rejected because he was a Bush rather than a Hornblower: someone who would not set the Thames on fire but could do many far more profitable and Christian things than that. I owe him a special debt of thanks because he organised a splendid celebration of the Silver Jubilee of my ordination. Then there was Elspeth Cornick, who was my secretary for most of my time at Aylesbury, taking on the job at financial loss to herself on leaving the employ of the Council. I am a very untidy person; so a good secretary makes all the difference in the world to my effectiveness. Elspeth was very good.

Des Harvey, our organist and choirmaster, was a constant source of strength. In addition to his musical and teaching abilities he was also an electronics engineer and got us fixed up with our induction loop which brought great joy to several hearing-impaired members of the congregation and to myself. He was the centre of a dramatic episode one Sunday evening. I'd just come back from a holiday and while away I'd left a notice at the back of the church asking people to write down any questions they'd like me to answer from the pulpit on my return. The idea was that such questions would be about the forthcoming stewardship campaign. To my horror when I picked up the paper one of the questions went something like this: 'Why doesn't our stupid organist make a better choice of hymns?'

Had I been wise I'd have taken this to Des and discussed the best way of handling it. But I wasn't and I didn't. Instead I decided I'd use it to pay tribute to Des and the Choir and say that I myself was responsible for the choice of hymns anyway, though of course that and other musical matters were discussed between us. The moment I read out that question Des stood up and, having announced *fortissimo* that he wasn't going to stay to be insulted, walked out. I don't think much attention was paid to the rest of the questions; so we came to the last hymn, for which I asked Dave Radwell, our assistant organist to play. He told me he didn't want to be a blackleg but after I'd assured him that after the service I'd be making my peace with Des he agreed.

As soon as I could get away I dashed off to Leighton Buzzard where Des lived and we were soon at peace. It was his wife Mary who gave us the quick settlement I'd hoped for. Des had begun: 'I'm not a touchy man ...', whereupon Mary roared with laughter. Des joined in a bit sheepishly and I was able to tell him what I'd said to the congregation after his dramatic departure.

It seems to me that the great majority of church organists are indeed touchy men and have a perfect right so to be. They have the power to ruin a service at any time and sometimes they must be sore tempted to express disapproval of the priest who may well be doing or saying things with which he or she is unhappy. Indeed I vividly recall a row between dean and organist in St Albans Abbey, when the organist demonstrated his wrath with everything that great organ could provide. Organists seldom have any security of tenure. Their congregations very rarely thank them. Many work entirely without pay; others for a pittance. Training choristers is a tough job. I'm told that even vicars sometimes forget the common courtesies and take their musicians for granted.

This incident brought back to my mind the sad events surrounding the end of Stanley Milnes's time as organist at St Nicholas' Harpenden. He was a lovely and much loved man and had done much excellent work but he was beginning to go downhill. Quite often he would accidentally drop an arm onto the keyboard and thus interrupt sermon or readings with a loud cacophony. So when in reply to criticism from the Church committee he said he'd resign I accepted that resignation at once. I wanted to see that he had a wonderful farewell with a really substantial thank you cheque. This never happened because he tried in vain to reverse his decision and mine and to stay on as our organist with the aim, as he himself told me, of finally dying at the console during a Sunday Eucharist. I feel I made the right decision but managed the whole affair badly. I did better at Aylesbury.

CHAPTER XXXVI

Although the resurrection of St Mary's, Aylesbury, was a most absorbing business there were plenty of other important things happening in my life at this time. Before any of the crises in the church began I had the privilege and joy of marrying our daughter Rachel to James Thompson, an art historian, whom she had met when he'd been at Oxford and caught up with when more recently she'd spent time in America. He came from Virginia and built a house near to his family on the Trail of the Lonesome Pine. It was a wonderful site but had one severe disadvantage, especially when it came towards the end of Rachel's pregnancy: this was that in order to reach the house one had to cross a railway line at an extremely informal unlevel crossing. 'So what?' you might ask. The problem was that coal trains a mile long used to cross their entrance very slowly; and worst of all they'd decide every so often to park right across it and take the weekend off.

Rachel wanted a church wedding not because she was an orthodox believer but simply because she felt that it would be serious in a way a register office ceremony didn't seem to be. I was happy to go along with that and Sylvia was very glad to be able to 'give her away', although we all knew she was her own person.

Through the generous good offices of Tim Harvey, who had been one of our churchwardens at Harpenden I got all the champagne and table wine we wanted for our wedding guests at shippers' prices. As a result of this offer we actually ordered twice as much as we estimated we would need and thus got ourselves quite a cellar-full of good booze which lasted us for years. Tim was an expert professional in the wine trade, whose expertise I'd sampled in the past.

Later I was involved in a minor way in Tony's wedding with Melanie. She belonged to the Orthodox Church and the ceremony took place in what was simply a large upper room in the priest's house. My job was to be a groomsman, which meant that for a long period I had to hold a crown above my son's head. We had plenty of incense and even a procession, though in that crowded space it lacked some of the dignity I'd come to expect from Orthodox worship.

Nevertheless it was a most joyful occasion and we hoped it would mark a change for the better in Tony's rather topsy-turvy life. He had suffered on and off from a fairly severe psychiatric illness. After leaving the Francis Bacon School, where he'd done brilliantly, he took a year out choosing to do Voluntary Service Overseas. In his interview for VSO, he was asked: 'Do you play any musical instrument?'

'Yes, the 'cello', he said.

'Oh, that's not likely to be much use', came the response to that. 'Do you play anything else?'

'Yes,' said Tony again, 'the double bass!'

'You'd better learn the guitar then before we send you out.' Which he did both speedily and to good effect.

So Tony went out to the Falkland Islands where he was a peripatetic teacher travelling round by sea, jeep, air and on horseback teaching from one to six children at a time in the various scattered farming communities. On his return he went up to Cambridge to read History but had an interrupted and difficult time because of illness. When he was twenty-one he did another voluntary job in troubled Belfast, working on a children's playscheme. Next he spent some of the summer camping in France, whence I was summoned to collect him from hospital and bring him home.

I was at a clinical theology annual conference, leading a small group, as was now my regular custom every August, when Sylvia got an urgent message to me to come home at once as Tony was ill again. For him and for all the family, particularly for Patrick, this was the start of a very difficult time. But we had been given a very positive prognosis by Dr David Watt, who was a personal friend and medical superintendent of St John's Hospital, Stone, of which I'd been a temporary chaplain. He said he was sure that Tony would ultimately make a complete recovery. Unfortunately that final recovery was not complete at the time of his wedding.

It was a great sadness to us – and, I suspect, to all involved – when this marriage, like Rachel's, ended in divorce. I have no answer to the problems these marriages posed. All I know is that Sylvia and I are incredibly lucky in that we have in the end learned to let each other be what we need to be and that we have four wonderful children who have gone through darker times than we ever did and are all now warm, outgoing, loving and much-loved adults.

Patrick in his turn suffered from a similar breakdown as had Tony but was over it much more quickly. In due course he got a job in the Social Services, for which high priority was given in the appointment to candidates for the post who had been patients in a psychiatric hospital. The illnesses suffered by these two sons made me sharply aware of my own manic tendencies, which I believe were inherited from my mother who was still running upstairs in her seventies and afraid she'd run out into the streets in her nightie when she was past ninety.

For some incomprehensible reason the Vicar of Aylesbury was regarded with some awe in the local community. At my first ecumenical meeting I discovered that when I gave my opinion on anything, that seemed to finish the discussion. The sense of the meeting was always: 'The Vicar of Aylesbury has spoken; there's no more to be said.' Maybe that tradition had been built up because discussion with my predecessor had been so difficult. The fact that discussion ceased did not mean that anything actually got done. It just stopped being considered.

On top of my parochial workload I was soon involved in committee work for the diocese. At first I enjoyed this, for it helped me have a wider view of what the Church was up to than I could have got from staying all the time in Aylesbury. However when I was asked by the bishop to join a new body he was setting up, the Oxford Diocesan Advisory Group for Mission, I said I'd only do so if he ordered me to resign from all my other diocesan commitments. I'm glad that he did this for me because ODAGM became an important part of my life. It was chaired by our beloved and splendid Archdeacon Derek Eastman. The extraordinarily competent Secretary was John Morrison, who eventually succeeded me as Vicar of Aylesbury. Most of the other members were distinguished academic theologians and we usually met in one of the Oxford colleges, in the rooms of Anthony Harvey at Queen's or Peter Baelz at Christchurch. The only major item I contributed to the group was a paper on the 'Non-verbal communication of the Gospel', of which I was rather proud but which was, I think, very quickly forgotten by all who heard it although it is as valid today as it was when I wrote it in 1976. The final paragraph went thus: 'In Jesus Christ we say the Word was made flesh. All too often in the Church the flesh is made words.'

The centrality of the university in the life of the diocese had considerable disadvantages as well as some benefits. That Christchurch College chapel should also be our cathedral always struck me as absurd and was the reason why I at first refused a canonry of Christchurch when it was offered me by the bishop. The whole realm of Practical Theology seemed to me to be a closed book to those in authority. This was emphasised for me when I was offered a sabbatical and chose as my project to do a term's study of Pastoral Counselling under Professor Howard Clinebell at the School of Theology in Claremont, California. Howard Clinebell and Charlotte Ellen, his wife, had become personal friends of ours through their close association with Frank Lake and clinical theology. It had been Howard's suggestion that I should come out and study with him but the committee which vetted applications for sabbatical projects turned this one down. As an alternative I came up with the proposal that I should study the continuing education of the clergy of the mainline Churches in the South Western USA. This was immediately accepted. Strange to relate Claremont's professor in charge of the continuing education of the clergy was none other than Howard Clinebell; so I enrolled in three courses relating to pastoral counselling and was assured by him that he would give me all possible help in my official project.

This was to be my third visit to the USA but my first to the West. Since 1956 I had been a member of the Fellowship of Contemplative Prayer (FCP) and had gone every year into retreat with that organisation, usually led by its founder, Robert Coulson, who asked me to lead a retreat for the American branch in Maryland in the summer of 1974. This was a great experience for me and it coincided with the approaching birth of Rachel's son, Luke, who eventually arrived 23 July. Sylvia had come over with me and had gone to visit a very old friend in Connecticut while I was 'witnessing', as we describe the retreat leader's job, down in St James, Maryland. During this trip I visited the old colonial town of Williamsburg, Virginia, and preached at Bruton parish church. After the service the rector introduced me to Gen. Robert E. Lee III, who was a grandson of the famous Civil War general. He in turn introduced me to Col. Robert E. Lee IV, who began by saying how much he regretted being unable to introduce to me his son, Cadet Robert E. Lee V, since he was 'at West Point right now'. I couldn't help wondering what a difficult life it must be for a boy born into that family even if he actually wanted to join the army.

Richard Stinson, who was Secretary of the American FCP group, had met me when I first arrived in the USA. Now his wife Anne met Sylvia coming down from Connecticut to Washington, DC, and we spent a brief but enjoyable time with them. From there we went together down to Virginia to stay with Rachel and James. Sylvia then stayed to see Rachel through her child-bearing while I had to get back to Aylesbury and work.

Michael Ballard, who was at that time Priest-in-Charge of St Peter's, greeted me with some interesting copies of the local paper, the *Bucks Herald*. I'd been away for four weeks and during that time I'd been the centre of that paper's correspondence columns. It had started with the anonymous letter I referred to above coming, I suspected, from a lady I knew well, which accused me of various iniquities, chief of which was that I was never in St Mary's but always off doing my own thing to the neglect of my parishioners and now actually living it up abroad. In the course of the following two weeks the paper was full of letters defending me, coming from Michael Ballard, Des Harvey and other members of the Church and also from a Roman Catholic who lived in St Mary's Square and commented that one of the things that gladdened her heart was to know by my ringing of the bell that I was in church praying for my people twice a day. Another letter said how proud St Mary's people should be to be able to share their vicar with people who valued his ministry in other parts of the world. I'm sure the whole episode helped me and the cause of regenerating St Mary's.

I suppose I wondered just a bit whether I'd come in for another dose of criticism when I was going to be away for four whole months and once again in America. In the end the only reaction I noticed was that I'd probably be leaving Aylesbury soon. Since I'd already started looking for a new job this was fair enough. I'd done a month-long course for senior clergy at St George's House in Windsor Castle and looked at several other parish jobs but always hoping to find something that would really make use of my counselling skills, which I was now determined to enhance in California.

Near the end of August 1980 Sylvia and I flew to Los Angeles. The local Episcopal Church was St Ambrose, which I'd agreed to serve in exchange for accommodation. The plan was that I would do most of the pastoral visiting and half of the Sunday services. There was no rector at the time and the Church was busy hunting for a new one. Like all the churches I came across in America, St Ambrose was wonderfully equipped and staffed. Later, on a visit to Pasadena, our host asked me, 'How many automobiles can you fit in your parking lot back home?' When I told him we didn't have any car park he went on to say, 'We can get twelve hundred automobiles into ours.'

St Ambrose did have clergy help from Dr Wappler, Dean of the Episcopal Students of the School of Theology, and of a non-stipendiary priest, who was a captain in the LA Police. It struck me as a trifle strange that among the clothes hanging in the clergy vestry during service times there would often be the policeman's accoutrements including, of course, a hand-gun. The church people were universally friendly and hospitable; the job was easy because all the dull jobs were done by the lay administrator and staff. I'd be told where I needed to go visit people and be given a description of who they were and how to get to them and that could mean a journey of up to fifty miles.

Once we were invited to come out for a picnic and were picked up at our door at around 10 a.m. After travelling some fifty miles our host said he'd have to turn back for a bit because there wasn't going to be another diesel station the way we were going and he'd be running out of fuel. So back we went for twenty miles, refuelled and were off again. During that day we drove through desert and up into the snow-covered heights of Mt Baldy. We had a super lunch and as it was dusk when we got back to Claremont, we went on to a restaurant and had a delicious supper before being delivered back to the rectory. I think we covered some 350 miles in all. We saw many wonderful sights and enjoyed extremes of both heat and cold. It seemed somehow to epitomise our whole Californian experience.

On the academic front things could hardly have gone better for us. Because of the research I had officially come for I was allowed to sit in on the opening meeting of the Faculty (the teaching staff) of the School of Theology. First of all I was personally greeted by the President who explained what I was doing and wished me success. Then each person in turn gave a brief account of anything of importance that had occurred in their personal life since the last meeting. One professor simply said, 'As you all, except Peter, know very well my wife died three weeks ago; and my heart is bursting with gratitude to you. There isn't one member of this faculty who hasn't either written me the most moving of letters or visited with me personally over this sad time. You are a great bunch.' He then wept openly for a brief while and his neighbours gave him gentle hugs.

Such openness would have been marvellous in Britain even in clinical theology groups let alone in an academic assembly. It was just the kind of thing I was aiming for in our Growth Groups and which I did ultimately find in various therapeutic settings. It also set the pattern for all the academic study that Sylvia and I got into. It was all amazingly informal. The odd thing when I look back on it was the sharp contrast between the kind of behaviour we enjoyed with our peers and our teachers and that which was enjoined on us in relations with our counsellees. All our counselling sessions were recorded, many with a video-camera operated by a fellow student. And I was on video once when I embraced a client, which I would often do in bereavement visits back at home. This however was strictly taboo; it led to my being severely reprimanded.

Under the conditions in which we worked the reprimand was thoroughly justified. Counsellors were always in danger of being sued by litigious clients, egged on by voracious lawyers – a situation with which we are just now becoming familiar in Britain but at that time almost unheard of this side of the Atlantic. Then there was the possibility that a counsellor would abuse his or her position of power to use a client to satisfy their own emotional or sexual needs. This was certainly a real danger wherever counselling took place; particularly since there were certain schools of thought in psychotherapy which actively encouraged behaviour they claimed as therapeutic while in fact it was abusive.

Another new thing we had to learn was what feminism had done to theology. God was no longer 'He', so one had to say such things as 'God loves God's world', which always struck me as ridiculous though I did come to see what they were getting at and had to acknowledge that our traditional way of thinking and speaking had been conditioned by centuries of patriarchal domination of women. At a lovely Thanksgiving dinner party we shared in there was a female Professor of Theology from New York who said she thought the best solution would be to call God 'She' for the next twenty years and then for the following twenty we could revert to 'He'.

After dinner at that party we were told that our hosts' custom on Thanksgiving Day was to have all their guests share whatever they were most thankful for in the year just past. This was another lovely time of open sharing, helping us to know the very best of American life.

With the help of introductions from Howard Clinebell I visited men representing the continuing ministerial education efforts of nearly all the bigger churches within fifty miles of Claremont. Virtually all of them had lessons to teach the Church of England. When I came to write up my conclusions about all this I thought the authorities back in Oxford would be impressed by my labours and do something as a result of my research. I did indeed get a pat on the back but as far as I know nothing whatever was done to implement a single one of my recommendations. Our post-ordination training was probably better than the corresponding work in the USA but it never exceeded five years (and in my case lasted just three). Where we stopped was where they really got going. Some ten per cent of our clergy persisted in their self-education. That was about the proportion of those in America who gave it up.

Of the four months we spent in the USA one was taken up with a tour which took us via friends in Pasadena and San Francisco to the Grand Canyon and the Yosemite National Park, which I feel must be one of the most beautiful places in the world while Grand Canyon is among the most awe-inspiring. We travelled by Greyhound coach, which would have been pretty comfortable if only other passengers could have stopped talking at night.

We got back to England just in time for Christmas, which we spent out of the parish, only getting back to work in time to see the new year in.

CHAPTER XXXVII

Since the vicarage front door was right on the pavement we probably received well above the average number of visits from wayfaring men who expected the clergy to help them. We had a policy of never giving money but always offering food and tea or coffee to such callers. Occasionally we felt abused by the recurring visits of one or two of these vagrants. One was particularly obnoxious because he showed no gratitude whatever for our help and yet kept coming back for more. On one happy day he paid us his final visit. It so happened that the doorbell was answered by our youngest son, Patrick, who, recognising our visitor, simply said (so loudly that we could hear him in different parts of the house): 'Fuck off!' Neither Sylvia nor I would have dared to express ourselves in quite those terms but Patrick's action was a great relief to us all.

On another occasion I answered the door to an Irishman, whom I invited in as usual. We gave him bread, cheese and tea and he told me a wonderful story of how he'd crossed the sea and come to Aylesbury to see his dying mother in Stoke Mandeville. He was now on the final leg of that journey but found himself without a penny with which to buy a little something for his mother. He told his story so well that I broke my rule and gave him £10.

Three days later I answered the door again to the same man, who this time was carrying a large plastic bag. As soon as he got indoors he said, 'Here ye are, yer Reverence. I pot yer tenner on a hoss and it came in fust. So I've brought ye yer share of the lute.' Out of that bag he brought a large joint of beef, a bottle of wine and a pound of tomatoes. We sat down and had a bit of a meal together and he went on his way rejoicing.

About a year later I opened the door to this same charming man who said, 'I suppose yer Reverence wouldn't think of lending me anither tenner?'

'You suppose right', I said, but he was of course welcome to come in and have another bite with us, when he regaled us with some good stories before leaving us for the last time.

Directly opposite our vicarage stood Prebendal House, which had now been bought, for some £100,000 I was told, by the Dowager Lady Roseberry, who lived at Mentmore, a vast mansion that eventually got sold to the followers of the Maharishi Mahesh Yogi as a centre for transcendental meditation. Since she was to be our nearest neighbour I thought it would be a good idea if I met her before she arrived. Since moreover I believed her to be wealthy and about to live next door to St Mary's I guessed I might well ask her to help in our money-raising efforts. So I wrote suggesting I call on her and she kindly invited us to lunch at Mentmore. In fact we lunched there twice, the second time with our daughter Rachel and James as well since our hostess had wanted to meet him because he was an art historian and she had plenty of artistic treasures to show him.

At our second visit she told us that apart from a few personal possessions everything in the house had now been sold and this even included a Woolworths waste paper basket that had gone for five times its purchase price. Buyers had come from all over the world for the auction, which raised several million pounds, indeed much more than was needed to pay off the death duties which had enforced the sale. She promised me that she would sell one of her pictures and give the proceeds to our appeal fund. She also accepted an invitation to come and have lunch with us at our vicarage.

The lunch was a bit of a disaster. Because she'd not been well and had a poorly tummy she'd brought her own meal with her. This of course was infuriating for Sylvia who had gone to great pains to produce a fitting meal. On top of that she announced that her car was stranded a little way off with a puncture which she'd be glad if I could fix for her. Then we had a nasty shock when her meal exploded with its beautiful china dish having accidentally slid onto a burner on the cooker. Not a good day, though the pre-lunch sherry had gone well with Elliott Viney and the redoubtable Miss Isa Duncan, lately Headmistress of the Prebendal School and the best teacher our Rachel ever had.

I'd asked my garage man to deal with Lady Roseberry's Rolls, which he did with promptitude but without thanks or payment from her at the time. This man was really quite a close friend by this time. He'd always looked after my motoring needs with great skill and on one occasion excelled himself. My Rover's accelerator linkage had broken and having got the car to my friend's garage he rang round all the Rover dealers and found that the connecting part we needed was no longer available. So he set to and made it himself while I watched him. It took about an hour and a half and when he'd finished and fitted it it was perfect. When I then asked him what

I owed him he said: 'Oh, I couldn't charge you for that. I've not enjoyed myself so much for years.'

Unfortunately my relationship with Lady Roseberry went a bit downhill after that and she never honoured her promise about the picture. After spending a great deal of money on the Prebendal she decided not to live there after all and sold it for something like £1 million. When next I saw her it was on the opening day of the Festival we'd organised to celebrate the reopening of St Mary's. That was 7 May 1979. The Rededication took place in the afternoon. Then in the evening we had a Gala Concert given by the December Festival Choir and the Milton Keynes Chamber Orchestra, of which Lady Roseberry was Patron. I greeted her on her arrival and she said: 'I bet you've never had as many people in here as you have this evening.' (There were about four hundred.) So I was quite pleased to be able to tell her that in fact, though I was naturally delighted to see so many people, we'd had many more for the Rededication service

Just up the road from us lived two sisters, maiden ladies who perhaps had better be nameless. They'd written a joint letter of complaint to the bishop about the reordering. Their complaint was that I was installing *toilets* in the church, which they thought was disgusting and a desecration of a holy place. The bishop sent the letter on to me with a copy of the one he'd sent to them. In my book the joke was that at about this time they'd informed me that they could no longer manage a church service because of their waterworks trouble. I used to take Communion to them at their home every month and we were always friendly at least on the surface, though I sometimes suspected that they didn't much like me. One day, when I'd just come home from hospital after some minor surgery, one of these ladies met me in the street and said: 'I hear you've been in hospital. What was the matter?'

I told her I'd had an operation on my genitals.

'Surely,' she said to my acute embarrassment, 'you can be more specific.'

'OK,' I said, 'I suffered from a hydrocele and had an op on my scrotum.'

'What's your scrotum?' was her next question.

'It's the bag in which I, like other men, keep their testicles.'

It's hard to believe this but her final question was: 'What are testicles?'

To which I replied: 'Balls. Good afternoon.'

As we parted I think she was murmuring, 'There's no need to be rude, vicar.'

The highlight of the week-long Festival was Graham Jeffery's production of Dennis Potter's play *Son of Man*, in which Graham played the role of

Jesus. It was certainly a far better production than the one I'd seen years before on television. Behind the scenes however it caused some ructions because the electricians who laid cables for the extra lighting twice over completely spoiled the working of the new organ, the magnetic force given out by their cables interfering with its electric action. The closing event of the Festival was an organ recital by Peter Hurford, who had been the cathedral organist at St Albans in my time there. It was through his good offices and experience that we got the organ builders to correct some defects which nobody up to that time had spotted.

In the autumn of 1981 when I'd just about given up hope of finding a new job that suited my counselling talents I was rung up by John Waller, now Bishop of Stafford. He wanted to know if I was interested in applying for the job of Adviser in Pastoral Care and Counselling in the Diocese of Lichfield. Once I'd made sure that my friend Ronald Smythe was no longer after it, as I knew he had been, I said that I was. So off we went to Lichfield where I was interviewed by a panel chaired by John Waller. The only part of that which I remember is a question put to me by Dennis Ede, who was Rector and Rural Dean of West Bromwich and obviously a leading light among the local clergy. He said to me: 'A parishioner of yours comes to see you and tells you he's going into hospital for a sex-change operation. What do you say to him?' I said I hadn't a clue and didn't believe in approaching people with words prepared in advance. My job was to listen and seek to understand and show I understood.

The committee was evidently satisfied that I would do but since no one had much idea of what the job should really be I was invited to work out my own job description in my first year. The reason they gave me for the creation of the post was the stress being noticed among the clergy and their families. Of course the job was not mine yet because we still had to look at the other part of it – the Rectorship of Elford. Sylvia and I were delighted with the house though we needed reassuring that we'd have central heating put in and a few other bits and pieces put in order for us. There was an acre of garden including part of the flood plain of the river Tame which flowed past the bottom of it, giving out a rather unpleasant odour which we failed to notice on this our first visit because the whole garden was covered in a blanket of snow. I was really pleased by the thought that we would be getting back to living in a village after eighteen years in towns. Elford looked good to us and we were at least not seen as too bad by the churchwardens whom we met there.

The last step in this process was my interview with the Bishop of Lichfield, Kenneth Skelton, who bade me welcome and said John Waller had assured him I was the ideal man for the job, which he was now glad to offer me officially. I accepted joyfully.

CHAPTER XXXVIII

There was a wonderful spirit in the renewed St Mary's and the number of worshippers continued to grow steadily. The exchange of the peace, which in some churches was so controversial, was quickly accepted and came in time to be perhaps too dominant a feature of our services: people would use it more to comfort the troubled and lonely and, regrettably, even to indulge in occasional bits of unloving behaviour. I'm sure that it did help isolated people to feel accepted. This indeed was very definitely one of the aims of my ministry. At one time I had an adult group preparing for Confirmation numbering thirteen in all, every member of whom was either divorced or in the throes of marriage breakdown. Most of them had been rebuffed when they had made earlier tentative efforts to join or come back to the Church.

Occasionally people complained about the unloving behaviour of some member of our congregation and since some of these criticisms were undoubtedly justified I had to say quite loudly and often that there could be no such thing as a wholly loving Christian community. What was happening at St Mary's must be true generally of any good Christian body: a genuinely loving Church was bound to attract the miserable, the outcast, the unappreciated and the unloved. Such new worshippers needed time before they in their turn were ready to attract others.

One of the saddest things about some forms of religion is the drive for purity; by which I mean the refusal to accept people who do not completely share the outlook of the 'management'. It seems terrible to me that so many Christians have a laager mentality; scared of those whose Christianity is at odds with their own, they build barriers where they should be breaking them down. In Northern Ireland we often see this polarisation and its dire effects; but on a less murderous scale the same attitudes bedevil many a Christian group in mainland Britain. I had a fierce desire to change this attitude wherever possible in the new sphere of work which I was about to enter.

During my last few months in Aylesbury I was dogged by further genital health problems, having had to have further surgery because of a botched job first time round and then prostate trouble, which led to my being offered a distant date for another operation. Since this was going to be very inconvenient I arranged to have my prostatectomy in St Luke's Hospital for the clergy in London. When a preliminary visit to the consultant there had taken place and a date in early April fixed, I rang up one of the churchwardens at Elford to inform him of the situation. To my amazement his wife, answering my call, told me that her husband was up at the church rehearsing with the rural dean for my institution. 'And when is that to be?' I asked.

'It's a fortnight today', she said.

'I'm afraid it isn't,' I replied, 'for I do have to be there myself and you seem to have chosen the very day I am to have an operation in London.' In the end it turned out that I didn't need the op after all. After I'd come round from the anaesthetic the surgeon told me it would be years before I needed it – if ever. He also warned me against having anything more to do with the surgeon who had messed me up over the last few years.

CHAPTER XXXIX

In April 1982 I started on my last full-time job. I'd decided that my top priority must be teaching the clergy of the diocese to be better pastors through the study of clinical theology. I sent out a letter to them all telling them that I would be available to help any of them or their families who were feeling stressed or in need of any kind of counselling or supervision of their own pastoral work and that they could trust any such relationship with me to be wholly confidential. I also wrote to all rural deans to say I hoped they would invite me to visit their clergy chapters so that I could get to know every ordained minister in the diocese. Further I said that I would be glad to run teaching days or evenings for any group of people who wanted to enhance their listening or other pastoral skills.

Looking at the tasks I faced, I decided that two-thirds of my time should be spent on the diocesan job and one-third on the parish. As in my last two jobs I was lucky enough to secure a very good secretary. This time it was Caroline Wiggall. For some of the time she brought with her a small daughter, Lucy, whom Sylvia cared for while her mother was working away in my office. The diocese also helped me a bit with such practical gadgetry as a large photocopier and my video-camera and allied equipment, which I found vital for my teaching work and for my counselling. This was nearly always video-recorded so that I could study sessions at leisure and show parts of them to my supervisor in the way that I'd learned in California.

One of my sadnesses is that I never managed to persuade anyone else of the value of video-recording, whereas I know that it proved most profitable in my own work. Frank Lake had taught his tutors the value of audio-recording their seminar teaching and I simply added to sound the extra dimension of sight. A counsellor can deduce much from the non-verbal language of a client which can easily be missed during the counselling session. When one or two members of a seminar group miss a session they are also able to watch the recording of it and so not miss out too much. Indeed I made it a condition of membership of such groups that they must watch the tapes of any missed session. I believe that this was invariably found to be invaluable.

Over my first two years on the job I got to visit the great majority of the clergy chapters and enjoyed these visits, finding a lot of enthusiasm for the kind of experiential learning that I introduced to them. In nearly every case I got the rural dean's approval to do some little exercise which got the members sharing at some depth with each other in a way that was new to the vast majority of them. Fairly often this led on to my running a training day for that chapter, which in turn might lead some of the members to enrol in the full length course in clinical theology.

In other dioceses the advisers doing my job mostly preferred to set up and run counselling centres; and I know some very good results were achieved this way; but my heart was set on improving the skills of those who were already engaged in the pastoral task and on getting more lay people trained in listening skills. I also did my best, without much success, to persuade my brethren in ministry that their work needed supervision. Over the seven years I was in the job I was asked some half dozen times to do a bit of supervisory work; and I doubt if anyone else was doing it. I myself was fortunate to find a splendid supervisor in Jean Way, whose psychotherapy practice was in Birmingham. I also took part in a *Gestalt* therapy group run by Barry Hinksman in Coventry. It was in this group that I really got in touch with the psychosexual problems of gays, lesbians and bisexuals and shed some of my long held hang-ups.

Not all my fellow clergy were well disposed towards me. I was most suspect in that part of the diocese that was furthest from Lichfield and I well remember one rural dean who, rounding off the meeting and thanking me for my input, said: 'Of course we all know that a good knowledge of the Fathers is all we really need in order to be good pastors.' I could thank God for Cuthbert Thicknesse and Frank Lake who had taught me in their separate ways to learn by doing and then reflecting rather than simply by reading.

By far the worst experience I had at the hands of my brother priests at a chapter meeting was at a far distant place of treasured memories from my RAF days. In church for a Eucharist and afterwards at breakfast I felt I was shunned. The crunch came at the meeting proper, for which I'd travelled some fifty miles and made a point of being present at their early worship. There was some business to be dealt with, which I'd quite expected. After this a long discussion ensued which was entirely focussed on the methods to be used to frustrate the will of the laity in the forthcoming meeting of the deanery synod. The whole point of these synods was that the clergy and laity should make decisions together and that if clergy wanted to meet separately they should not try to do business that belonged to the synod. It seemed to me that in this deanery the clergy saw their people as mindless and often hostile sheep who had to be shepherded into paths they disliked. I found the discussion nauseating but felt I should probably hide my feelings at this juncture.

When at last this business was complete the rural dean introduced me to the chapter in some such terms as these: 'We have just fifteen minutes left before I close the meeting during which time we hope Peter Graham can justify his existence to us. I have to say that we were unanimously opposed to his appointment, being all of us convinced that the only proper job for a priest in the Church of England is in the parishes. We feel no loyalty whatever to the diocesan centre at Lichfield. They demand our money and inflict on us officers we don't want. In particular we didn't want you. So now it's up to you to convince us that you have something to offer us and if we ever invite you to come here again we shall expect a blow by blow account of the benefits you have secured for us.'

That of course is not a verbatim report but is how I heard it and can hear it still. Comparing it with my interrogation as a POW in Dulagluft I'd prefer the earlier experience every time. I don't think I made much of a job at replying. At least there was no threat of handing me over to the SS! I just came home rather despondent. In fact this encounter was not wholly in vain, for some time later I got a cry for help from one of the priests who'd been there, which of course I was delighted to give, though the first thing I had to do for him was to assure him that I'd not breathe a word of his 'treachery' to any other member of his chapter.

I found much in common with the other diocesan officers and a good deal of training work was done in cooperation with them. A group of us organised experiential training and much progress was made. Geoff Babb, whose hearing was even worse than mine, encouraged me to stand up for myself in situations where previously I'd been a sort of wallflower because I couldn't follow what was going on. I found the diocesan work most fulfilling but decided that I'd retire soon after I reached my sixty-fifth birthday, when I would qualify for my Church pension.

The fact that I'd just announced my impending retirement coincided with a storm that arose locally around issues of homosexuality. It was really set off by an article the bishop had written for the diocesan journal. Of course it got banner headlines to the effect that, according to him, all homosexual acts were sinful. I was sure this wasn't exactly what he'd meant but felt that this statement was very damaging to my own work and, more importantly, to many gay and lesbian people who were doing their best to live Christian lives surrounded by prejudice and misrepresentation. I simply don't believe that because a person's orientation is other than straight they must lead celibate lives for ever. I knew also of gay priests who did in fact live as celibates but who might well have non-genital relationships with friends of their own sex. Therefore I wanted to have the whole issue thrashed at a bishop's staff meeting. This happened. I opened up the subject in fear and trembling but discovered that nearly everyone present was with me. Throughout the diocese people were asking for guidance and many were not liking what was on offer.

At the end of it all I had a short but wonderful session with the bishop, who is a very understanding and loving man. He shared with me his own perplexity and the pressure he was under to say the sort of things he had said. By now it really had come home to me that it was great not to have had to endure the burdens of being a bishop.

Being Archbishop of Canterbury must be even harder. At the Lambeth conference of 2000 it was impossible altogether to avoid a showdown between those (largely African) bishops who wanted to hold to the traditional condemnation of all sexual relationships outside heterosexual marriage and their liberal opposite numbers. The result could have been a lot worse; for the assembly did at least agree that the voice of lesbian and gay Christians should be listened to even though the old rules still applied. I doubt however if much listening has been done by the great majority of conservative thinkers. Their argument has always been that the Bible clearly condemns homosexual behaviour, by which they really mean anal intercourse. They ignore the contradictions in their position. The principal text they quote is from the mosaic law which says (Leviticus 20:13): 'If a man also lie with mankind, as he lieth with a woman, both of them have committed an abomination: they shall surely be put to death.' This sentence of death is also to be carried out on any man who picks up sticks on Saturdays (Numbers 15: 3 2 –6). Getting away for a moment from sexual acts to sexual orientation the Bible has plenty to tell us about that great Old Testament hero David, whose love for Jonathan was 'passing the love of women' and about Ruth's relationship with her mother-in-law Naomi to whom she swore 'The Lord do so to me, and more also, if ought but death part thee and me.' Whatever may possibly have been right in those ancient conditions, much of that law certainly cannot be applied to us in our time.

The Apostle Paul clearly condemned all homosexual behaviour but his comments on the subject are so illogical that all we can tell for sure is that he was as homophobic as they come today. Jesus himself had nothing to say on the subject but it's crystal clear that he spent most of his time in the close company of men and that the disciple whom he particularly loved was John.

For many years I have seen it as part of my task to help my fellow Christians to rid themselves of the old prejudices and learn at least to accept that a Christian could legitimately hold the views I hold and that setting out to 'cure' those whose sexual orientation was a minority one was almost certainly a stupid and often positively harmful thing to do. Of late it has been paedophiles who have been having the hardest time of all. We do need to be clear that some people are fixed in a position where their only sexual attraction is towards children. That makes them paedophiles but not necessarily abusers. A man who finds himself thus attracted needs all possible help and support in resisting the temptation to use children for his gratification. It is a very hard thing for him to do because he often honestly believes that he is doing only what the child concerned would like him to do, which may in extremely rare cases be true. Whatever may be thought about other sexual orientations, I have no doubt that paedophilia is a severe handicap. Those who suffer from it and strive to resist their impulses have the same kind of struggle on their hands as has the dried out alcoholic but any lapse is likely to be far more devastating to themselves and to others.

Before my departure from the job I did my best to see that clinical theology was carried on and enhanced in the diocese. At that time I had a waiting list of over fifty people who hoped to join CT seminars and I was supported by seven other trained tutors. My main hope was that another CT person would be my successor. Gerald Hughes who was at that time Chairman of CTA and a brilliant educator was looking for just such a job as mine and would certainly have applied for it but for the fact that I had to warn him off in the knowledge that the diocese would not consider appointing a man who was divorced and remarried however brilliant and well qualified he might be. Brian Cox, who did in the end succeed me, was also a CT-trained priest and did some very good work, doing better than I had in the parish too; but sadly he fell ill and had to take early retirement.

CHAPTER XL

Our actual arrival in Elford was auspicious: more like Harpenden than Aylesbury. On our first full day at the rectory we were visited by Pat Hodgetts who informed us he was a local farmer and Chairman of the Housing Committee of the Lichfield District Council. He had brought us a sack of potatoes as a welcome gift and said: 'You can always count on me to give you any help I can; but don't ask me to come to church.' On my first Sunday he was there in the front row of the church, where I could count on his presence as much as on that of anyone else there. He was also Chairman of the Governors of the village school, a body to which I also came to belong. He was a far more effective school governors' chairman than I'd ever been and though almost dictatorial in a kindly way he did this job as he did many others in a way I could only admire.

Back in Aylesbury I suppose my method of chairing St Mary's PCC was not dissimilar, for John Bush once said: 'Peter Graham is completely democratic. He knows exactly what he wants done. We discuss the issue thoroughly. It's put to the vote and then we agree to whatever Peter wanted.' I can't say it went like that with Elford's PCC. I certainly didn't get everything I wanted but we had a good relationship and I had to accept that Elford people were more conservative than any I'd pastored before.

They gave us a wonderful reception in the parish church at my institution when it did at last take place; and Sylvia was brought right into it and given her own warm welcome. We loved our house and garden and I personally was glad not to be faced with the sort of financial problems I'd had over the previous nine years.

We arrived at a time of political controversy about the Falklands War. Maggie Thatcher was at the pinnacle of her new-found popularity so it was hardly surprising that when I voiced my opinion of her in the village shop I could no more be believed than when I spoke out against her in Zimbabwe on a visit to my Zimbabwean brother. I admit I was overlooking some good things she'd done when I said I thought she was possibly the worst Prime Minister we'd ever had, but I was sickened by the mindless jingoism which had saved her political bacon just as I was cheered by the straightforward Christian sermon Robert Runcie preached at the Thanksgiving service when the war was over. I'd spent most of my life, including my service career, seeking to promote the social gospel – the good news being not a matter just for individuals but for creating what Jesus called the Kingdom of God, the establishment of right relationships and brotherhood everywhere. That is why few pronouncements from on high so enraged me as Maggie's: 'There's no such thing as Society.'

One of the problems in country parishes is nearly always centred on the relationship between those who'd lived all their lives in the area and the incomers. I remember once talking with a couple of old ladies who were feeling most put out because some newcomers were serving teas at the church fête. They, the old ones, had done this job for years. They were well past it now but felt they should have been asked to do it all the same. I once asked a certain Dora Thompstone, whom I'd got to know well chiefly because her sister was crippled with arthritis and was one of those to whom I took Communion at home, about some matter of local history, concerning which she was unable to help me. So when I next met him I asked the same question of Cyril Gilbert who was, I believe, the oldest inhabitant. I also told him how I'd failed to get the answer from Miss Thompstone. 'Dora Thompstone!,' he said, 'she's a newcomer. I remember her coming – nineteen hundred and four!' You might think that I, who had arrived in 1982, could never possibly have been counted as an Elfordian but the clergy are usually exempt from the general prejudice against incomers. I must also make it clear that I never felt there was actual ill-will between the various groups in the village, whereas back in Eaton Bray it was sometimes so bad that it nearly led to murder.

We enjoyed warm relationships with many of our parishioners but none better than with the first one we'd met on our arrival. Pat Hodgetts had endured two bereavements during our time at Elford, losing his first wife Mary and his son Eddy. He'd been as good as his word about helping me in a number of practical ways including help over the visual aids I came to use virtually every time I preached in the parish church and arranging the ploughing of the bottom part of the rectory garden. He'd also shared our house for a time with Jill, his second wife, while their new home was in building. As a result he almost certainly under-stood my job better than anyone else in the place. It was Pat who made our farewell party in the village hall into something truly satisfying with a lovely speech of appreciation of Sylvia and me. Most touchingly Caroline Wiggall's little daughter Lucy burst into tears and said 'I don't want you to go.'

CHAPTER XLI

During our last three years at Elford we'd spent the best part of two holidays hunting for a retirement home. We wanted to live in a village and be reasonably central for our descendants.

Michael and Jill lived in Lancashire, Rachel in London, Tony and his family on the Isle of Wight and Patrick in Cardiff, where he was soon to marry Gill, who was not a small person in any sense of that word. The wedding was in the Friends' Meeting House in Cardiff and was a simple but very moving ceremony in which both Michael and Rachel spoke of their love for him and Tony demonstrated his by getting there with his daughter Zoë in atrocious weather, which had involved a horrid Solent crossing.

We looked briefly in Gloucestershire, where Sylvia had two lots of relatives, then in West Hampshire, where we found the prices too high for us. We peeped into East Devon but found nothing to our taste. Finally we concentrated on Somerset and Dorset. We'd almost given up hope of finding what we really wanted and had settled on a house in Somerton, which we thought far from ideal, when we visited an estate agent in Sherborne to ask them to do a survey of this property for us. 'By the way,' I asked as soon as we'd sat down, 'I suppose you've not got anything yet yourselves in our bracket?'

'Sorry, sir, nothing doing, I'm afraid', the agent said. Then a voice piped out from the back of the office: 'I beg your pardon, sir, but something's come in by this morning's post that might suit the Grahams.'

That something turned out to be Carrier's Cottage, Buckland Newton, which we went out to see there and then and subsequently purchased. Our hearts sank a bit when we first saw the cottage empty and discovered that we'd have to spend so much on it that the total outlay would far exceed the limit we'd set on the purchase price. We'd looked at the church and its notice board which told us that they had services both traditional and modern. I'd also 'phoned the rector to find out if there were any bread and breakfast places we could use when visiting our cottage. He was David

Hopley and his reply was 'No, I can't help you there because of course you'll come and stay at the rectory.' This we did and so got to know and love David and Liz; just as later on we were to get to know and love the village as a whole and its many friendly people.

David insisted that if I wanted to conduct services in any of his five churches I was not to be a blackleg, by which he meant doing the job without payment. This suited me well as I'd no intention of ending all paid work. I planned to go on teaching clinical theology, to do some counselling and perhaps some supervision. To the tax man I called myself a Pastoral Consultant and I was prepared to give my services free as a CT tutor and charge other clients £20 an hour or £100 a day.

When we finally arrived at our home it was to find we still had no roof, nor was the internal plastering finished, nor the painting, though there had been more than a year in which all the planned work could and should have been done. We got straight down to doing that part of it (£5,000 worth) which I'd a bit rashly undertaken to do ourselves. Most of that got done in the first three months. Some of it is still not done after thirteen years.

I got the backing of my new diocese and was able to set up a CT seminar in Sherborne, assisted by Katy Kayes, a Roman Catholic, who gave me splendid support and continued to co-tutor with me until just before she died. She brought with her a tremendous extra bonus in the shape of her husband John, a retired pharmacist who for several years operated my video-camera for me, thus greatly enhancing its value. Eventually he was to take a share in the actual teaching.

I also got all the counselling work I could cope with, for which I was lucky enough to find a fellow resident of the village to supervise me. On top of this I was invited to become the supervisor of the counsellors at Post Green, which was a job I loved, though I sometimes felt that I was less competent than those I was supervising. However that really didn't matter because the supervision was basically a peer effort with me acting as chairman rather than sole teacher and I did have some gifts that I could share.

For my own inner well-being I belonged to a group analytical group for some ten years. This was the most valuable of the many groups I'd belonged to in my adult life. For half that time Sylvia belonged to it as well, which meant that the lengthy car journeys were enjoyable too. We met four times a year from Friday afternoon to Sunday afternoon usually in Oxford but occasionally in other places. We were led by two conductors, Hymie Wyse and Brian Maxwell, to both of whom we are deeply indebted.

Because of the confidential nature of such groups I can say little about this experience. For me one momentous discovery was the identity of that poor small boy who in my first term at Teddy's was gang raped. Many of my experiences and feelings over the fifty-five years since then made sense in a new way. My abject terror in that Liverpool pub for instance seemed more natural in the light of my particular trauma in that distant past when I'd been not just an observer but the victim. For all of those years I'd said nothing to anybody about that time. Even Sylvia was completely in the dark about it but this isn't as strange as one might think because I was so deeply in the dark myself.

Owing to the kind of work I've been involved in over the last part of my life I've had to give a lot of thought to issues around repression and now believe that it's a wonderful mechanism which often preserves our sanity. When long-repressed material comes bubbling up into consciousness it's good that we should be with caring people and that we should be mature enough to face something that in the past just didn't bear thinking about. For years in all sorts of therapeutic groups I'd insisted that I had had a near perfect childhood and therefore couldn't compete for attention with other people whose traumas were so much worse than anything I'd known. Now, while I know how lucky I have indeed been in my parents, my wife, my family, my friends and my counsellors, I am also aware that I have had my share of deep pain and have learned all too well how to bury it.

The most persistent area of pain has been around my hearing disability and I still find it hard to fight my corner and persuade people to stop mumbling and hiding their mouths from me. Sometimes it's other people's embarrassment that causes trouble. Soon after my retirement I appealed to the War Pensions Agency for an increased pension in line with my increased deafness. I was directed to a local independent audiologist, who did the usual tests on me and who was clearly required to fill in a questionnaire about me. Glancing at this document, he asked me what I felt was the principal difficulty I had on account of my disability. I said I was clear about that: it was that, while still sexually active, I could no longer exchange whispered sweet nothings to my wife when making love in bed, where hearing aids can't be worn.

When I came before the tribunal at Exeter a month or so later the chairman asked me a few questions and then said 'There's a blank space in this audiologist's report: nothing here about your principal difficulty. Don't you have one?' I remembered that man's blushes and repeated what I'd told him. The chairman who was a retired senior RAF officer said he fully appreciated what I was saying.

Next he asked the woman representing the War Pensions Agency to make out her case for denying me the increase I was seeking. She spoke in a low voice and fast. When she was done the chairman asked me if I could follow what she'd said. To which I replied that I couldn't hear a word of it. He then said to her: 'Madam, Mr Graham has a hearing problem, which I have not. Even so I found it hard to follow you. Would you now therefore present your case again at half the pace and twice the volume.' The poor woman was clearly distressed by this and made a poor fist of her prepared speech. The outcome of all this was that I got a bigger increase in my disability pension than I'd dared hope for.

I had even greater difficulty in persuading the agency to pay for me to have the most up-to-date hearing aids and three times had to fight to get them.

Buckland Newton is a very different kind of village from those we'd lived in at earlier stages of our lives, chiefly because nearly all the inhabitants are newcomers. We'd only been here for a month when we became distributors of the local newsletter and one month further on I'd been asked to be treasurer of the village hall committee. We are surrounded by many friendly people here; so much so that we can't bear the thought of retiring away to a more protected environment for our declining years. We've looked elsewhere but decided that here is where we want to stay. I shall go on doing a bit of counselling work while it is still possible and leading worship until I'm warned off doing it. Both Sylvia and I are beginning to feel our frailties a bit more and I'm aware that my body is quite looking forward to its final departure.

Shortly before he died in April 2001, we received from Val Rogers, our very old friend from Haileybury days, a poem that says quite marvellously where I am now and rejoices in our destiny.

Soul to Body

Said soul to body, 'Why so sad
At all that ought to make you glad:
Failing powers and sleepless nights,
Sloth that with your vigour fights,
Hands that once grasped rock now cramped,
Lively spirits hourly damped,
Legs that levered you on high
Over the rocky ridge of Skye
Now unnerved, as good as dead
Painfully twisting in the bed.
Arms that once embraced your love
Scarcely now empowered to move,
Fingers that once could music make
Crippled now to shrink and shake,
All these imagined ills are gains!
All changes come through present pains.
The gasping of your failing breath
Portends the chrysalis of death;
But that once past, you then will be
A fitting dwelling place for me,
Freeing me from my present thrall
Tied to a dead animal;
Now ageless, sinless, strong and free,
All that a body longs to be,
Transformed, renewed and full of light,
A temple for my own delight,
Where you and I at last will be
At one throughout eternity.'